The Patient
Has the Floor

ALISTAIR COOKE

The Patient
Has the Floor

Alfred A. Knopf New York 1986

THIS IS A BORZOI BOOK PUBLISHED BY ALFRED A. KNOPF, INC.

Copyright © 1986 by Alistair Cooke
All rights reserved under International and Pan-American Copyright Conventions.
Published in the United States by Alfred A. Knopf, Inc., New York, and simultaneously
in Canada by Random House of Canada Limited, Toronto.
Distributed by Random House, Inc., New York.
Library of Congress Cataloging-in-Publication Data
Cooke, Alistair.
The patient has the floor.
I. Title.
AC8.C6495 1986   081   85-45704
ISBN 0-394-50365-1

Grateful acknowledgment is made to the following for permission to reprint
previously published material:

"The Patient Has the Floor" by Alistair Cooke, from the *Mayo Clinic Proceedings,*
February 1966, vol. 41, No. 2. Reprinted by permission of the Mayo Foundation.
"Thoughts Coming Out of the Ether" by Alistair Cooke, from the *Royal College of
Surgeons of England Annals,* 1976, Vol. 58. Reprinted by permission of the Royal
College of Surgeons of England.
"Hypochondria: The Layman's Specialty" by Alistair Cooke, from the *Royal College of
Physicians Journal,* London, 1973, Vol. 7, No. 4. Copyright © 1973 by Alistair Cooke.
"The American in England: Emerson to S. J. Perelman" by Alistair Cooke, a Rede
Lecture published by The Syndics of Cambridge University, 1975. Copyright © 1975 by
Alistair Cooke.

Manufactured in the United States of America

FIRST TRADE EDITION

A SIGNED FIRST EDITION OF THIS BOOK HAS BEEN PRIVATELY PRINTED
BY THE FRANKLIN LIBRARY.

TO

Dr. Robert Woods Brown

FOR

ENCOURAGEMENT AND FRIENDSHIP

Thanks are due, and are hereby tendered, to the persons and institutions that gave me the opportunity of airing my prejudices: the Mayo Clinic; the Royal College of Physicians; the Hon. Carl Albert, former Speaker of the House of Representatives; the Folger Library of Washington, D.C.; the Philadelphia College of Physicians; the English Speaking Union (twice); former President Kingman Brewster of Yale University; the Royal College of Surgeons; the United States Military Academy; the British Medical Association; the Philadelphia Bar Association; the National Trust for Historic Preservation; and the Senate of Cambridge University.

Contents

Listening to speeches is a sometime duty which very many intelligent people rightly dread or, at best, put up with, as they put up with Christmas shopping or going to funerals. As one who spent thirty years or more "covering" political rallies, I share the general dread. But as a practicing word man, learning throughout half a century to write for listeners as well as readers, I came to wonder why so few public speakers appear to have stopped to consider the peculiar fun and challenge of a face-to-face appeal to the humanity of a captive audience. Maybe there is a built-in tribal suspicion of the very act of speechmaking, possibly going back to a child's healthy distaste for sermons (two of which I had to endure every Sunday) or tedious after-noons memorizing such orations as Antony's over Caesar's corpse, the main lesson that came through being the showiness and hypocrisy of speechifiers.

Yet speechmaking is an art form, just as the novel, the sonnet, the essay, the broadcast are art forms, all worth a lot of attention and scads of practice. When Shaw, whose slightly querulous Dublin voice and chop-chop delivery made him a rather poor public speaker at the start, was asked how he later learned to develop a pungent speaking style, he said: "You learn to speak in public exactly as you learn to ride a bicycle: you keep falling off."

Before the invention of the microphone, it was necessary to learn, as singers learn, to project from the diaphragm, and the unnatural effort of this must have had much to do with the ponderousness, or the overblown emotionalism, of what was being said. In all the years that I have stalked politicians, I can think of only six who I felt had perfectly acquired the knack of accommodating their gift of the gab to a particular audience.

Lloyd George was the first, at a time when a speech had to be audible to a large audience in an auditorium, or a public square, or to the small but formal audience of the House of Commons. He was a master of the required projected style who knew how to float dirigibles of real, or artificial, indignation and light them up with flashes of wit and sarcasm. It was remarkable that his speeches often read poorly in print. The same could not be said of Churchill, who had only one, majestic style—of rolling Gibbonesque cadences punctuated by short, sharp Anglo-Saxon idioms—that he used as much for a breakfast monologue as for a heart-rending appeal to the American people to "give us the guns and we'll finish the job." In him, before an audience of six or six million, it was the timing of the vernacular punch and the pawky humor that kept people alert who were otherwise unimpressed by the rumbling procession of Latinisms.

Hitler I heard before a small outdoor crowd in Munich at a time (1931) when he was regarded by the rest of Germany as an eccentric radical or a failed rabble-rouser. To attract an audience of a hundred or so, he had the staff of the Braunhaus shut their desks and whip outside to form a claque. A small ambulance standing by seemed another unnecessary come-on, but at the end of the twenty-minute speech I heard, two or three women had fainted, for the good neurological reason that he could hypnotize even a small audience with omens of a dire future. He did this not with the hysterical bawling which was all we saw in the newsreels before and throughout the Second World War but with a style of the most artful variation of mood, from tenderness to whimsy to outrage. He convinced me, for one, that we had had it.

Franklin Roosevelt overlapped the two eras of the soaring public speech and the microphone talk, and, unlike the hundreds of politicians who loved him or loathed him, he learned wholly different techniques for the massed crowd at the Capitol and the family settled before a loudspeaker. Ronald Reagan learned (how slowly and painfully can be gathered from seeing his films) that the microphone is a speaker's best friend, to be charmed, solaced, moved by an acquired natural speaking style, so that all his speeches, however inflamed with emotion, sound the way he might sound if he were tearful or cheerful across a small room. By contrast, few politicians even today appear to trust to the invention of electricity, and consequently sound as if they were addressing a PTA meeting or a rally in Madison Square Garden.

The last, and not the least memorable, of this sextet is the late Senator George Aiken of Vermont, a dry, wry, hilarious after-dinner speaker, whose relative ineffectiveness in the Senate must have been due to his conviction that audiences of any size, indoor or out, were in fact a small bunch of cronies sipping their coffee.

M Y own case can be simply stated. If the microphone had not become a standard adjunct of ballrooms and auditoriums, there would have been few speeches and no book, since a radio engineer once told me that I had a pair of lungs of the lowest decibel volume he had ever monitored. Towards the end of the Second War, I was attached for a spell to the U.S. Air Transport Command as a correspondent-lecturer, and had a humbling baptism before pilots, navigators, mechanics and other grease monkeys crowded into gymnasiums, or out on the tarmac, in most of the ATC's American bases from Detroit to Brownsville,

Texas, to Great Falls, Montana. These "show me" skeptics were not there to be harangued about the beauty of Anglo-American friendship or the holy Christian mission of the Allies. They wanted as much entertaining sense as possible to be packed into the fewest possible words. It was an early, good reminder that your audience is just as sharp and sensitive as you are. On these talkative safaris, I learned too that the microphone enables a speaker to talk to an audience of two thousand with the same ease of emphasis and timing he would use before an audience of two.

For about twenty years after the war, I was on the lecture circuit and spoke ad lib before every sort of audience in most states of the Union. Then, in 1965, came the invitation from the Mayo Clinic. It was followed by other invitations from other distinguished medical bodies. By the time the House of Representatives got around to requesting a celebration of its two hundred years of boisterous health, I had gone "off the platform" but resolved thereafter to accept only invitations from learned bodies about whose specialty we laymen on the outside have firm and quirky convictions they may be unaware of. So that is what this book is about: the layman talking before the College of Cardinals, a chore for which—as I explain in the title lecture—the journalist ought to be particularly well qualified.

At any rate, I felt the time had come to say where I stood on some of the issues that spark our prejudices and engage our lives, and about which—since nobody is going to elect us to the Senate or compel us to testify before a congressional committee—most of us can afford to be cheerfully dogmatic or offhand in the social banter of friendship. Several friends urged me to include a lecture I did in Brussels in 1983 before an audience of NATO and other Western ambassadors and their military attachés. It came down in the end to attempting to say how we could melt the frozen conflict between the United States and the Soviet Union. I found that I could not, and still cannot, say what should be done about the nuclear buildup, arms control, and the rest of it, except to plead for a fresh start in which both nations would sit down and trust each other. Since we do not trust each other, I—like some very eminent persons, I may say—was simply announcing the problem rather than solving it. So that speech had nothing new to offer, and was quietly discarded.

All these lectures except one were reprinted in the appropriate journals, together with footnotes indicating sources, which professionals should readily track down, but which, I believe, would only distract and irritate the general reader. The exception was the keynote lecture I gave in San Francisco to the assembly of double-dome British and American scholars looking into "the state of the language." My mock-modest suspicion that my contribution was "so humble that it may affront many people here" was well founded: the sixty following lectures appeared in a book carrying the title of the conference, but not mine. The pain of this slight was greatly relieved by congratulatory notes from Graham Greene and Philip Larkin.

I would not claim that these attempts to beard the experts in their sanctuaries did much to revolutionize the relations between the doctor and his patient, the architect and his trusting client, the soldier and the civilian. But from much subsequent mail, I gathered that some professionals had registered a twinge of guilt or self-knowledge. Anyway, for me, the speeches constituted invigorating exercises in an ancient and honorable form of social contact.

The Patient
Has the Floor

The Patient Has the Floor

GIVEN BEFORE THE ANNUAL CONVOCATION OF THE
MAYO GRADUATE SCHOOL OF MEDICINE, ROCHESTER,
MINNESOTA, MAY 28, 1965

The Patient Has the Floor

I'm sure that Dr. Johnson—your Dr. Johnson—gave me an unintended opening when he wrote to invite me to be your speaker and added: "You may discuss any topic of your choice; although all of us in Rochester who are involved in this program are primarily in some branch of medicine, we do not necessarily expect an address related to medicine. Any topic of broad general interest would be suitable."

This is, I imagine, the usual courtesy offered to pacify the fears of some statesman, lawyer, or other grandee who never appears before a doctor except to have his chest tapped, his knees jerked, his tongue depressed, his innards photographed, his rectum proctoscoped, and all his juices filtered, measured and pronounced upon. It is, though you may not know it, a permanently humiliating relationship: I mean the relationship between doctors and the rest of mankind. And it is because most people do not care to bring it up in public that I believe it might be useful for me to do so.

In fact, I think it is my duty as a journalist to speak *for* the patients to *you*. Because a journalist has always been the social link between the expert and the layman, between the public and the private man. At his worst he can become the publisher's disciple, the politician's yes-man, the tycoon's sycophant, the actor's press agent. But at his best he reports the world not as it ought to be but as his eyes and ears tell him it is.

Because our only relation with our doctor occurs when we need him badly, we must all, for our self-respect, adopt in a mild form the delusion which every young mother hugs to her person: the belief that her obstetrician is the only man who has ever safely delivered a baby.

So I speak up for the patient, because the patient, when you see him, is usually too terrified to speak up for himself—I mean too terrified to speak about doctors. The raw material rarely answers back, which is what makes laboratory research so satisfying. But if the Mediterranean fruit fly could talk it would doubtless acquaint the farmer with some of his misapprehensions. The dolphin, whose whistles and grunts constitute a pretty sophisticated language, is already beginning to make us look silly. It is just possible that the layman, the patient tottering wide-eyed into this strange jungle of viruses and cultures and men in white, may see a few simple things which you do not see.

May I give you an instance, which happened the only other time that I dared to appear, so to speak, as a lay preacher before the College of Cardinals?

A few years ago, I was invited to Boston to speak at the annual dinner of the Massachusetts Heart Fund. I was expected, as I understood it, to launch the drive and supply, if possible, a slogan. When I arrived I found, to my embarrassed astonishment, that all my dinner companions were eminent heart specialists, including Dr. Paul Dudley White, who—you may recall—preserved General Eisenhower.

My qualifications for addressing a distinguished body of heart surgeons and probers were hardly less pathetic than they are for facing you today, although my two closest friends at Yale were medical students who are now a surgeon and a psychiatrist of alarming distinction (whom I would still not trust to lance a boil or wipe a tear). I began to try and justify my being there by noting that a foreign correspondent is a man whose very employment requires him to keep up the bluff that he takes all knowledge for his province. So I shuffled in front of the doctors samples of their own jargon. I don't suppose I fooled any of the formidable men present. But even the most disinterested specialist in any country takes on the prejudices of his own land. And my own peculiar history—that of an Englishman born and bred, and an American tamed and naturalized—had forced me by accident into a peculiar specialty of my own, which is the continuous observation of what is British about Britain and American about America.

So facing these tolerant, though solemn, medical men, I took the risk of recalling that the United States is at all times a country with a passion for fashion. By which I don't mean it has a fetish for women's clothes (which country does not?)—I mean its ears are alertly tuned for the last cry in every kind of process: the latest trick in bookbinding, or tree-planting, or bridge-building, or teaching piano, in bathroom gadgets, in theories of education, in cocktails, sex, architecture—in ideas.

All I could offer the doctors was the reminder that this trait extends also to the learned practice of medicine. I recalled how, in the 1930s, every rash or sneeze was attributed to an allergy and a roaring business was done by manufacturers of flockless pillows and proprietors of Canadian resorts above the ragweed line. And so it went—down to that memorable evening before the heart specialists, which I dwell on because it explains why I am here, and some of its lessons may apply to us.

At that time, the word "cholesterol" gibbered through the land as the word "unclean" used to herald the approach of a leper. There was a tremendous to-do about the lethal snags created in the bloodstream by carbohydrates and animal fats, either separately or in combination. Four or five years ago it was established, at least to the satisfaction of a panicky populace and the makers of anticoagulant pills, that cholesterol was as fatal as silt along a riverbed and was responsible for most of the seizures and strokes of what are called successful men (that is, men who decide to take a first trip around the world and then keel over at their desks).

I gather that this precious discovery is now not only in doubt but is looked on by some specialists as a naive superstition, a hangover from the Dark Ages of medicine (namely, the 1950s). The rush to consume only soybean and vegetable fats was declared to be premature. *But* carbohydrates are now more suspect than ever. So there is a national retreat from pastries and a grateful stampede back to beef, and lately, a learned pamphlet advises me, back to alcohol.

All I could say to this medical gathering was that if the cholesterol theory was true, and if animal fats and carbohydrates were certain prescriptions for heart attacks, then they would have to explain the miracle whereby fifty-five million Britons were still alive. For of all known civilized communities the British are the connoisseurs of animal fats and the compulsive addicts of carbohydrates—with their morning toast and eggs bubbling in bacon fat, their biscuits at eleven o'clock, their lunch of more meat and potatoes and (worse) suet, then tea and more biscuits and cake, and dinner and meat and bread again, and potatoes and pudding—and perhaps an emergency snack of cheese and biscuits to guarantee coming safely through the night. How to explain the endurance, the ignorant but cheerful survival, of the British?

I saw that the doctors were now tense and puzzled, which is always a sign that you have a specialist by the tail. I was bold enough to offer an answer. Britain, I had noticed, maintains rights-of-way across fields and meadows and builds footpaths alongside highways, and uses the phrase "Let's go for a walk" almost as an idiom. In America you cannot walk across fields except in pursuit of a ball with a liquid center—and there are no footpaths once the town ends. The British walk, and cycle and walk, even in the rain. Let us face it, gentlemen, I said— "they function!" Could it be, I wondered—like Harvey groping towards the theory of the circulation of the blood—could it be that lumps of cholesterol could be shaken loose from the walls of the arteries by a lively bloodstream, as rocks and weeds are carried away by a river in flood? Perhaps the secret of avoiding blood clots lay in the humble admonition of the London bobby: "Keep moving!"

After this barefaced performance I sat down in some embarrassment until Dr. White told me that I had spoken words of the profoundest wisdom, and that he wished the slogan "Keep moving" might be taken over and plastered on billboards throughout the United States. I told him it was not copyrighted but the trick would be to get the American population to learn, as a novelty, the very old process of walking to work, or simply upstairs.

The vainglory of this occasion came back to me when you flattered me with the invitation to be here today. I don't expect, and you shouldn't, any similar moments of clairvoyance. But sometimes the patient who doesn't know what ails him can help the doctor find out by merely reciting his gripes and grievances.

I have two. And they are the minor and the major themes of this talk.

The first is the subtle tyranny of fashion, even in the sciences, even in medicine. I have already suggested that it is worth any doctor's while to pause from time to time and ask himself whether he's really pursuing a new and fruitful line or whether he's running with the herd; whether he's falling back on a well-worn conviction or whether he's falling back on a national prejudice, or even a prejudice of the school he was trained in. Edward Rist in his essay "What Is Medicine?" noticed that "in every country our colleagues have their phantoms and their ghosts. For the Englishman it is uric acid, for the German the exudative diathesis, for the American focal infection."

It is simpler even than that. I have noticed in knocking around the world, and getting the same (the traveler's) complaint in several countries, that doctors, however circumspect, tend to take on the folk prejudices or habits of their country. Thus in France, every stomach upset is at once attributed to a malfunction in that ole debbil liver, which all Frenchmen alike regard as the most vulnerable of all human organs. They consequently soothe the stomach with bowls of vegetable soup and a glass of wine three times a day. In Germany, they administer first a black draft and then having tapped the belly with a wooden hammer to see if it gives off a tremulous hollow echo, they put you on black bread, chicken broth, and charcoal. In England, they instantly prescribe a bland—(not to wander around in search of a finer word)—a bland diet of tea, blancmange, and bread soaked in hot milk. In Scotland, I am glad to say, even eminent gastroenterologists order up a soothing draft of milk and whisky, the milk (a rather toxic fluid) being cut down and cut off as the patient improves. In America, the patient is abandoned at once to bouillon and Jell-O; and to *ice water*—to which, by the way, the British ascribe all American afflictions from peptic ulcer and coronary thrombosis to shortness of breath, sinusitis, and the existence of the Republican Party.

Now let us go to the main theme, which is about the dangers and the dullness of professional jargon: the use you make of the language that we—the doctors and the patients—have in common. What I want to do this evening is to make a plea to you as professionals whose main business is to restore men and women to their normal place in society (that is to say, whose professional aim is—as old Adolf Meyer said about psychiatrists—to bow out of the lives of your patients as soon as possible), I want to ask you to come halfway to the patient in explaining to him health and disease. In other words, this is to be a little lecture on jargon, offered to a profession that is more prone to it than most. Why this should be so I have been unable to work out. In my boyhood the most practical aim of learning Latin was to help you employ as little Latin as possible in the use of English. If you know the roots of a word like "circumlocution" it is then easy to see that the English word is "roundabout."

A few years ago I had a lively argument with a French journalist who started reciting to me all the English and American writers he had decided wrote badly. I couldn't guess his criterion until he mentioned that none of them "wrote like Dickens." I told him there was no compulsion to *do* that. He was astonished. He explained at elegant if laborious length that in France there was really only one acceptable prose style, outside of the argot and vernacular of farm and city life. The style had been established in the eighteenth century, if not earlier. Molière wrote it, Flaubert wrote it, so did Victor Hugo and so did President de Gaulle. I am happy to say that he was even more astonished when I told him that the beauty of English was its resilience, its great variety, the fact that it could embrace—and rejoice in—the styles of Dr. Johnson and Art Buchwald, of Chaucer and Henry James, of Dryden and H. L. Mencken, of John Milton and James Thurber, of Hemingway and S. J. Perelman, of Bernard Shaw and Peter De Vries, of Mark Twain and the King James Bible.

You may say that you are not in the business of style. May *I* say that you are in the business of describing as precisely as possible what is happening to a man, woman, or child who seemed to be healthy and is now certainly sick. I truly believe that the best doctors are trying with all they have to practice and vindicate the scientific method, which I take to be *the effort to find a generalization that covers all the known facts.* There could be no nobler aim in science or in writing. You are, in fact, faced with the central problem of style, which is to say as cogently as possible what a given audience can understand. When it is brilliantly done in medicine you have, by your own admission, the classic descriptions of disease—Buerger, Osler, Freud on the central nervous system, a mere journalist (I am proud to say), Defoe, on the signs and symptoms of the plague—even though he was too young to have witnessed it.

It is always a hard task, but I'd like to elaborate on the fact that it is not peculiar to medicine. When something is exactly analyzed, and the definition is stripped to the bone, it is always memorable, which may be why centuries of students have memorized the propositions of Euclid. For when Euclid says "the angles at the base of an isosceles triangle are equal," it stays said. Very often the thing defined is something that's been noticed for generations but never said so well. Aristotle was the first man to notice that "a play tends to have a beginning, a middle, and an end." This sentence guaranteed his immortality for over two thousand years.

I think one thing that holds good medical men back from the attempt to translate their jargon into Anglo-Saxon is the fear that they will lose their academic standing and become known as popularizers, which among American scientists is a horrid word implying a degradation of truth in the interests of fat royalties, public popularity, or an invitation to appear on television. God knows we have as many of these fakers among doctors as we have among the hyperthyroid members of the clergy. But because something is done badly is no reason why it should not be done well. A Frenchman has told the history of the world more lucidly in a hundred pages than Sandburg can tell the history of Abraham Lincoln in four verbose volumes. We are short, and, in an age of mass communications, pathetically short of good, let alone great, popularizers. I am sorry to have to say that I think the British have been in our time, and before our time, more concerned with the effort to reduce their professional longhand into the universal shorthand of the common speech. For classic examples we need go no further than one family and read T. H. Huxley on the habits of the ant or the butterfly and Julian Huxley on the biology of the penguin.

I know that most of you have not the time to say in two hundred words what the *Journal of the American Medical Association* manages to say in two thousand. I respect the scruple of any professional man who refuses to fall into slaphappy generalizations for the sake of simplicity. Where it is a matter of life and death, or even of pain and discomfort, it is better to be accurate than lucid. But what I am saying is that, given a simple fundamental change in medical education, or rather a fundamental supplement in the early days, it would be possible for many more doctors to be both lucid and accurate. Suppose that a first-rate teacher of the English language gave regular courses to medical students during their internship—or, better, that there was always someone on hand to translate into English the parts and functions of the body at the moment a student was learning them, so that he discovers why fingerbones are called phalanges, because he is reminded of the array of a Greek phalanx; and he learns also that lumbar is simply a "loin"; then the day might even come when doctors would talk to patients about collarbones instead of clavicles and admit to a scared patient that an edema is nothing more or less than a swelling.

If this happened, who—you may ask—would be the gainer? The answer is, you and the patient and medicine; because the more you tried to talk in sensible monosyllables, the more— I think—you'd find yourselves getting to the root of what was wrong and what was right. I certainly believe that if medical students were compelled to spend some time of every week translating passages from the *Journal of the American Medical Association* into English, they'd be surprised to discover how much of the professional jargon simply said the same thing over and over (or in a complicated way said nothing at all), how many of these learned men had the gift which Winston Churchill attributed to Ramsay Macdonald "of compressing the smallest possible amount of thought into the greatest possible number of words." I think, if you try out these little translation experiments for yourself, you will find that your work will be quickened by a directness and informed with a healing humanity, for which none will be more grateful than the patients. And let us not get too solemn about what is meant by humanity: it ought always to mean compassion, but it might also include humor, which dignifies both the giver and the receiver and is an excellent medicine in itself.

Before I started a trip around the world a doctor said to me that I ought—and I quote him—"to equip yourself with appropriate cathartics and also with some handy provision against dysentery." He was really not saying any more than a friend of mine, a layman, who only a few days later gave me the essential advice for all travelers in distant lands. "You've got," he said, "to load up with stoppers and starters." If I may say so, I am often struck, more often in America than anywhere else, with the contrast between the vivid and honest accuracy of the vernacular we all use and the often elephantine jargon of the specialist.

Jargon, too, is often a cagey, noncommital attempt to walk all around the object. I mean this with all respect to anyone sweating to work his way through to fundamentals. When you really are unsure about a function or a process, you tend to get lost in a maze of protective adjectives and in many abstractions, which are the linguistic elements of cloudiness and fog. Soon the jargon, if repeated often enough, is doing the thinking for you. As a man who works at a bench with words, I sometimes look back over my daily pieces to try and spot words or expressions that I am using too often; for of course there is as much jargon in politics as in anything else. On the New Frontier, nobody decided anything; they made "a determination" or "a judgment." "Task forces" were called on to prepare "position papers," until it was seen that a task force was no more than a committee trying to see where we stood. In the Great Society, wars are no longer extended or spread but "escalated," causing the British cartoonist Osbert Lancaster to show a gentleman of the old school remarking that "since the Costa Brava is becoming so crowded in July, I hope the movement will not escalate to Frinton-on-Sea."

I am not saying you should drastically reform the *Journal*. It's your playground and you should be allowed to have fun in it. I am not saying that you should not use "ilium" and "tibia" among yourselves, but the patient will probably feel more relieved to know that all he has is a pain in the pelvis or the shinbone. Of course, the impulse towards jargon is very much a matter of character; and it's likely that you can no more cure a naturally pompous person than you can reflower a virgin. So that you won't think I'm attributing indigenous pomp to the medical profession, let me give you some melancholy proof that the jargoneer appears in all walks of life.

Road builders, you would think, would be more down to earth than other men. But in California a low bridge is not marked as a low bridge. It is "impaired vertical clearance." The gerontologists are in league with the real estate men to disguise, among other facts of life, the unavoidable one that we all grow old. So that an Englishman arriving in Phoenix, Arizona, and asking for the famous old folks' home is met by stony looks and directed to the "senior citizens' retirement community." In the United Nations, there are no longer the rich and the poor, though the most menacing social fact of our time is that the rich countries are getting richer while the poor countries are getting poorer.

But the poor will not be called poor; after a few years they resented being called "underdeveloped"—they are now known as "developing."

Shall we now take a look at your own beloved profession? Briefly, for it is a painful experience, and this should be a joyous occasion. I am looking at a piece in a recent issue of your favorite journal about which jobs produce anxiety in the young. At one point the author reveals "the finding that occupation-related emotional stress may play a more significant role in the causation of coronary attacks in young persons than heredity." I take this to mean that the stresses of particular jobs may cause more heart attacks in the young than heredity. Next the author says: "To determine whether or not such a gradient in coronary heart disease prevalence does indeed exist . . ." This can be accurately translated as "To find out whether this is so . . ." What did he do? He, as he says, "conducted a survey in selected types of employment which differ significantly with respect to tensions created by routine demands of the job." In other words, he decided to look into certain jobs that seemed to induce more or less tension in the young.

He had his troubles, especially with the questionnaire: "It is recognized," he says, "that certain weaknesses are inherent in the questionnaire method of survey, chief of which is the unknown prevalence of disease among nonrespondents." (You can never know how sick are the absent.) Finally, he produces this pearl: "Moreover, this method does not provide data on deceased subjects." This great man has discovered not only that dead men tell no lies—they also answer no questions.

Once, just before the construction of the floating harbors that were to be used for the invasion of Normandy, the Admiralty officials sent a note to the Prime Minister asking permission to start building at once. First they explained the job (pardon, the project) in elaborate language, and then wrote: "Permission is urgently requested for the immediate implementation of this directive." Mr. Churchill sent the request back with a note in the margin: "If you mean should you build now—do it—*carry on!*"

Ladies and gentlemen, do not equip yourselves with appropriate cathartics. Get some starters. Do not contrast living humanoids with "deceased subjects." Study rather the quick and the dead. Do not implement a directive, ever. Carry on!

Hypochondria:
The Layman's Specialty

THE LLOYD-ROBERTS LECTURE, GIVEN BEFORE THE ROYAL
COLLEGE OF PHYSICIANS, AT LONDON, DECEMBER 19, 1972

Hypochondria:
The Layman's Specialty

I did not pluck this title out of the air. No professional writer, even when he is invited to address a distinguished body, is going to lean back airily and wonder what might amuse or instruct them. He is usually preoccupied with some opus or other, and what he tends to give is nothing tailored to the appropriate specification but a chunk of the work in progress. What a lucky thing it was, then, that the college's invitation should have come to me when I was sitting in the apartment of an old friend of mine, a doctor, in San Francisco. He was, for the first time in many months, relaxing. Not because the load of his hospital work was any lighter than usual. But one patient of his had just gone off, at his urging, on a month's holiday to Europe and she had left him with at least one hour a day to himself. She was not, you understand, seriously ill. The question was, and had been for several years, whether she was ill at all. But she is a veteran hypochondriac with the temperament of Job and all the frailty of Boadicea or Queen Victoria.

We were going over her case and wondering how to incorporate its clinical contradictions in a book that he and I were then beginning to sketch out, a handy manual on the very theme I have dared to choose for this lecture.

Anyway, I had in my pocket the college's invitation and I

turned to him and said, more in alarm than modesty, "Why me? Why should the Royal College of Physicians turn to me, when they might have invited Linus Pauling to recount the conquest of the common cold with vitamin C?"

"Because," he said, "they're taking no chances. They know that Linus Pauling is probably going to be the first human being to die of the common cold. On the contrary," he pointed out, "you have been getting along for years with spastic colon, diverticulosis, an inflamed duodenum, and an interesting history of urticaria pigmentosa, not to mention varicose veins, frequent muscle spasms in the lower back, flat feet, and a tendency to argue with yourself when alone. This meeting of theirs is two years away, and you are quite simply a better medical risk." He also added, "When you consider that most doctors figure to spend between 40 and 50 percent of their practice on hypochondriacs, and your friends must tell you things they do not tell us, then practically any layman—and, for heaven's sakes, a reporter—ought to be able to contribute something. Go ahead," he said. And here I am.

First I should like to relieve you of the fear that I am going to try and tread in your angelic footsteps. Or to go over the ground, the unflagging battleground, where the vigorous ghost of Dr. Freud disputes with his followers and renegades whether hypochondriasis is a distinct syndrome, an entity, or a symptom. I leave it to you to line up for the next year or so legions of poor guinea pigs to be weighed in the nine scales of the Minnesota Multiphasic Personality Inventory; or to follow up those 181 docile patients who trooped through the Maudsley Hospital and waited six years to hear whether they were hypochondriacs or psychoneurotics. I fancy that many of those research subjects must have been only slightly elated to hear that at last they were carrying the proper label. Some of them, I imagine, must have felt much as I did when after I'd been promised by a surgeon that after a subterranean operation I'd feel like a new man, I felt like the same man but very itchy. I went back to him after some weeks and he said, "Well, everything fine?"

"No," I said, "everything is not fine, I'm scratching my tail off."

He made a careful examination and came up with a triumphant smile. "Nothing to it," he said, "it's simply post-hemorrhoidal itch."

"Don't name it," I said, "cure it."

Nor do I propose to rebut or support the very belated assertion of a Seattle psychiatrist that "the time has arrived when the psychiatrist should have equal time for his opinion on the contemporary practice of medicine. The pseudo-clever sayings of the physician and surgeon at the expense of the psychiatrist have wide currency and may do harm." I can only throw in the tentative comment that, from a cursory review of much of the psychiatric literature on hypochondriasis alone, it seems to me they have been at it for quite a time. And as for our right to pseudo-clever sayings at the expense of the psychiatrist, I can only suggest that God did not give psychiatrists an exclusive license to make remarks about human nature. Plato, Joseph Addison, Benjamin Franklin, Laurence Sterne, and Smollett, to go no further, have all made observations about hypochondriasis and the practice of medicine that are not at all pseudo-clever. They happen to say in sharp language what much of the psychosomatic and sociological literature says in monographs as interminable and dense as a traffic jam. As two examples only, I give you Franklin's "Nothing is more fatal to health than an over care of it." And Laurence Sterne's "People who are always taking care of their health are like misers, who are hoarding a treasure which they never have spirit enough to enjoy." Compare these shrewd remarks with this gem: "The authors did not find that the isolated patient used his physical symptoms to promote social interaction with medical personnel."

Jackson Smith, looking into the even more tortuous body

of psychiatric literature, makes the interesting observation that "psychiatrists tend to be more tolerant of the hypochondriac than the rest of us." They should be. If they play their cards properly, they can have him for life. May I say that as a generally unrepentant Freudian, who believes that the profoundest psychological discovery of the past century is that in the unconscious opposites are the same, I do not wish to take pot shots at the psychiatrists from the safe bivouac of a camp of physicians. But a psychiatrist deciding to examine hypochondriasis might do well to remember the venerable Edward Glover's suggestion to psychiatric interns that in their training analysis they ought to ask themselves why they chose a profession in which they will always be right at the other man's expense. And there is also the point that a classical analyst, even if he watches over a patient for as long as ten unproductive years, is one of the few medical men unlikely to be threatened by a suit for malpractice.

There is only one arena in the field of professional research on hypochondriasis into which, as a layman, I dare to rush, not so much with a dissent as a pair of raised eyebrows. It seems to me astonishing that down the years, you could almost say down the centuries, from Benjamin Rush in 1812 to W. H. Gillespie in 1928, and even into our own time, the doctrine should still persist that there is a fundamental distinction between the male and female hypochondriac, that the male is a compulsive-obsessive neurotic, whereas the female is an hysteric. This has got to be true only in the literal sense that women have wombs. It seems to me to be an interesting example of the male chauvinism of the Greeks, and our long dependence on their language as a descriptive tool of medicine. I do not see why a chronic hacking cough when the winter comes on, a fear of airplanes, the instinctive conservatism of doctors in politics, in fact all the protective hypochondriacal behavior with which a man or woman reacts to the threat of change, should not be put down as an hysterical reaction in both sexes. That doctors are not immune from hypochondriasis had never crossed my mind until I came on a paper, in the *New England Journal of Medicine,* about the special hypochondriacal leanings of medical students. Hunter, Lohrenz, and Schwartzman describe the process as follows:

> The following constellation of factors, occurs regularly. The student is under internal or external stress, such as guilt, fear of examinations and the like. He notices in himself some innocuous physiological or psychological dysfunction, for example, extrasystoles, forgetfulness. He attaches to this an undeserved importance of a fearful kind usually modeled after some patient he has seen, clinical anecdote he has heard, or a member of his family who has been ill.

When I mentioned this, with eyes bulging, to my San Francisco colleague, he said, "Students, hell. How about the hypochondriasis which chooses a medical specialty?"

"How come?" I asked.

"Well," he said, "dermatology is a famous sanctuary for people who are too nervous even to attempt a diagnosis."

I was even more puzzled, but I should tell you that this dialogue came about because I had suddenly developed brown spots on both legs, just above the sock line. They itched; clearly I am an itching type. Anyway, the affliction completely baffled him. He settled for bedbugs, but there was something abstruse about this complaint that did not satisfy him. Then something struck me. I had been deep in the Nevada desert, and I mean literally, walking across a petrified stretch of the Humboldt Sink, to reenact the ordeal of the Forty-niners over the unavoidable, dreadful stretch of the walk where they had to go sixty-five miles without water. I asked my friend if he had ever read any of the Gold Rush journals. I remembered, then, that one of the daily irritations they took for granted as they came onto the alkali desert was something then known as "alkali itch."

"Well, I'm damned," said my doctor. He gave me a cortisone ointment and within days it improved dramatically.

"Thank God," said he, "we don't have to call in a dermatologist."

"Why so?" I asked.

"Well," he said, "to quote the great Dr. William B. Bean, 'I share their confusion but not their nomenclature.'"

I pressed him with mounting enthusiasm for other examples of hypochondriasis among doctors. He mentioned "anxiety" as a key word and reminded me that after a bout of diverticulitis, I had been scrupulously scrutinized by a proctologist who subsequently gave me a diet of things I should never eat or drink again. It ran to two single-spaced typed pages, and I saw myself for the rest of my natural life reduced to the gruel and graham cracker diet of John D. Rockefeller, without—alas—his millions. My friend looked at this list and tore it up.

"Forget it," he said. "All proctologists are spinsters, and that's where they think the Communists have been hiding all this time." (I found out for myself that the only proper diet for diverticulosis is strictly to avoid all those things you don't like.)

This is not the place, and I am not the type, to go into the monsters of hypochondriasis who are too tragic to be funny, though I think we should all pay tribute to the really splendid case of Mrs. M., reported by Dr. Paul David of the Chicago Medical School. She must be the reigning empress of hypochondriacs. Beginning in 1953, with an amoebic infection, she was apparently cured by cortisone but complained that it had "shocked her system and changed her metabolism." She thereupon insisted on being proctoscoped three times a week (maybe she, too, thought she was harboring a Communist), and from then on, for the next ten years, began to shop around. By 1963, she was regularly visiting the GI clinic for colitis, the metabolic clinic, the allergy clinic for multiple allergies, the neurology clinic for numbness in her right arm, the dental clinic for a small node under her left jaw, the medical clinic for regular checkups, the chiropody clinic for an ingrown toenail, the ophthalmology clinic for pain in the left eye and a granular eyelid, the ENT clinic for difficulty in swallowing, the cardiac clinic for a flutter, the orthopedic and arthritis clinics because the X-rays of the lumbar spine revealed osteoporosis, the dermatology clinic because her hair was falling out, the surgical clinic for a small nodule on her right arm, and the gynecology clinic for a Pap smear. She is, need I say, still in rude health. And may I now make amends for my earlier sideswipes at the psychiatrists. She was referred to the psychiatric clinic, was delighted to add another to her list, and one year later had shed all her afflictions and now requires an occasional Alka-Seltzer.

Having put my toe into the deep water at your end of the pool, may I now retire to the shallow end, where even an amateur may wade, pausing along the way only to say that the technical literature warms a layman's interest only insofar as it comes close to the perceptions of the greatest of modern diagnosticians of hypochondriasis. I mean the late Stephen Potter. I therefore bow gratefully in the direction of Dr. Asher for his analysis of the Munchausen Syndrome and Dr. Edwin Clarke for his happy coining of the Hospital Hobo, of whom Mrs. M. is a superb example.

So now I dare to add a note of my own, which may be naive but may with luck contain one or two of those forgotten obvious truths which tend to issue from the mouths of babes and sucklings. I hasten to accept my San Francisco friend's cogent observation that a reporter and a doctor have, or ought to have, something in common, namely, a habit of observation. I say a habit and not a gift, because even when it is inborn it has to be developed. In fact, I believe I turned into a reporter because of an early fascination with Sherlock Holmes and the later luck of being the son-in-law of a very distinguished epidemiologist, who enthralled me when he recounted the sort of detective work involved in the isolating and naming of tularemia, or the famous plague of amoebic dysentery at the 1933 World's Fair in Chicago (which turned out to have come from a single barrel of infected oysters shipped a thousand miles from a seaport town in Maine, delivered to a single restaurant in Chicago, and served between certain hours on a single evening). Even though I have now retired from the daily grind of a reporter whose job is not to say how the world should turn but how it does, I cannot overcome the reporting habits I picked up long ago.

I had better begin by following the prescription of Henry Plummer, novel in his day, of a family history. My father was the hypochondriac in the family. He expected the human body to work to perfection every minute of the day. His happened so to work, but he started in early manhood to study dietetics. However, he did not let his studies interfere with his natural tastes, which were those of any ordinary Lancastrian born a hundred years ago. A half-dozen oysters for breakfast, moving on to fried bacon and eggs, and fried bread, a pot of tea, a loaf of bread and marmalade, and—after three intermediate meals, all fried—winding up at ten p.m. with cake, cheese and biscuits, and an appalling brew called "coffee essence."

My father, at the age of forty-two, turned green one afternoon and fainted. He was convinced that the end had come and went into total despair for twenty-four hours, after which he reverted to his normal blooming health for the next forty-two years. In old age, he put it down to being a nonsmoker, a teetotaler, and the swigging of a morning saucer of Kruschen's salts. It never occurred to him that a daily walk of ten miles and an incorrigibly cheerful temperament might have had something to do with it. By the way, he had a tremor of the hands all his life, and the mere mention of a doctor made it worse.

My mother, on the other hand, was a very tough invalid

for her eighty-six years, begin possessed of a splendid constitution and appalling bronchia, which produced terrifying daily
coughing fits, any one of which would have made my father
drop dead out of sheer fright. And yet my mother, who lived
on the assumption that serious illness was what happened to
her friends (which indeed it eventually did), was completely free
from personal hypochondriasis. I say "personal" to distinguish
her from what might be called the *folklore hypochondriac*. She
believed everything the neighbors told her. And in her childhood
she had evidently been told plenty, such as that open windows,
and drafts sneaking under doors, cause pneumonia. This is a
folk belief especially strong in the North of England, though I
regret to say it stops short at the Scottish border. The result was
that our living room, like that of most other North of Englanders
I knew, was kept at about ninety degrees, with clamped windows
and a roaring fire. To this upbringing I ascribe my pleasure at
living in American houses, where Dickensian mists do not per-
vade the dining room, where also you take a bath (in the bathroom) without the remotest awareness that the outdoor tem-
perature is ten above zero, where people never seem to have
heard the British axiom that whatever is uncomfortable is good
for the character.

I did, however, pick up most of my mother's medical cautionary tales. Sitting on wet steps was a certain recipe for piles.
As soon as May was out, you threw off your undershirt and
braced yourself against an Arctic June. The general misunder-
standing of the tense of the verb in the folk saying "Feed a cold
and starve a fever" meant that at the first sneeze you were fed
like an elephant, and if a fever appeared, you then went on a
starvation diet.

The folklore hypochondriac more than most, I think, fights
a winning battle against his intelligence. My mother was an
intensely intelligent woman and witheringly observant about

human frailty (in other people). But at the first hint of a thunderstorm, the first darkening of the sky, she would retire under the nearest table with the family cutlery.

I do not know how I got through all this but I suspect that the mechanism of a temperament that overcomes its environment is but little understood. I had the strictest Methodist upbringing. I was assured early on that hellfire was an actual postmortem sauna, reserved for people who swore, drank spirituous liquors, played cards (except whist, which was then respectably in fashion), or went with girls. But I went with girls from the age of four, and if that was a premonition of hellfire it was very agreeable indeed. I hazard a clinical guess and put it down to an actual split in my father's personality between what he, a lay preacher, had been taught and went on teaching and the contradictory truth, as he couldn't help noticing it: as, for instance, that godless men were often kind, that some people who drank were very affable, that many an adulterer seemed to be having a good time. In other words, and in the teeth of everything he had learned and thought he believed from the Old Testament and the New, he really held Mr. Justice Holmes's view of truth: "That which a man cannot help believing must be so." In his case, he could not help believing that his observation was better than his instruction, that life was nothing like so miserable as his spiritual teachers had insisted.

On the other hand, many hypochondriacs cannot help believing the worst. Or let us say that there is the *fatalist hypochondriac,* who takes an instinctively dramatic view of life and therefore believes in instant cures and instant damnation. In my observation, this type is very common among theater people; and I have noticed a striking sympathy between their view of health and their view of politics. The people who hear that a man is going to have an operation and immediately conclude he has a malignancy are the people who also immediately conclude that proof of a bribe taken by a government official shows that the whole government is corrupt; or that Mr. Nixon's visit to Peking will permanently soften the Chinese.

I suppose most laymen, and possibly a few doctors, still think of the hypochondriac as a melancholy person, because we are prejudiced by the literal definition that that is where depression and low spirits came from. But let us now consider the bounding or *smart-aleck hypochondriac*. He keeps up with the latest cures, for he has always something to cure. He keeps up with the latest illnesses, and takes vigorous steps to combat them. There is a new drug, and in acquiring it he conveys that medicine has been floundering in a dark tunnel since Hippocrates and has at last seen the light. He usually has a passionate belief in vitamins, following their miraculous progress through the alphabet. One year it is C, the next D, now E. He ridicules the doubts of any layman; and his doctor, if he is wise, does not tell him that he cannot build up an inventory or storage battery of vitamins, that if he takes four hundred units a day of vitamin C he will use five of them and pee 395 away. These smart-alecks are often very healthy people, but only, they assure you, because they religiously observe a regimen: fifteen minutes' jogging, two dozen deep breaths, two sets of vitamin pills at intervals, and honey from a special farm in Canada or Norway. And they have discovered a pharmacopoeia all their own.

This brings up the question, which is presently seizing a committee of Congress and the officials of the Food and Drug Administration, of how much people should be left to medicate themselves. In a recent hearing by the FDA, one of its medical men, attacking the idiotic medicine which most people learn from the telly, said that his agency had listed over a thousand across-the-counter drugs that are suspect in the sense that most of them are totally ineffective and some of them are harmful. But to prove it, the FDA would have to bring several hundred test cases before the courts. And he figured that each one would take, on appeal, about three or four years to settle.

I myself believe that the telly and the miracle ads—short of propagating actual harm—are a boon and a blessing to doctors, for most people everywhere practice self-medication until the symptoms grow alarming. And human nature being what it is, the chemists (and especially those knowing pharmacists who are physicians *manqués* and love it) save doctors from queues of people who, if they were more intelligent and less gullible, would clutter doctors' consulting rooms from dawn to midnight.

These erudite findings will conclude on a note which sounds ever more resonantly as people get along in life: hypochondriasis in marriage. I would like to look at a couple of variations on what might be called the *supportive hypochondriacs.* Dr. Jackson Smith has graphically described the case of Mrs. Wilma S. and her immortal husband George, who takes her tenderly to the doctor week after week, year after year, for her headache. He is as much concerned when she hasn't got it as when she has. For George was "never comfortable around women unless he could help them," provided he was not called on to fulfill the most obvious marital requirement. Wilma appreciates his boundless consideration, especially in the matter of "letting her alone." And, says her doctor, "George is intuitive enough never to let his joy over this arrangement shine through."

The first variation that occurs to me is the *martyr hypochondriac,* most often the wife, though, in time, women's lib may drastically change that. She is apparently devoted throughout a long marriage but is never free from several chronic ailments. Suddenly, if she's lucky, she becomes a widow. Her symptoms vanish, she takes off; she, who had been a housebound housewife, takes up the cello, goes to the theater, rustles up old female companions and goes to the mountains, or the West, or Europe. She blooms, she puts on weight or takes it off, according to whichever she had regarded as her lifelong problem. I have only very rarely known a widow who did not take a new lease on life. This may go to show that inside every devoted wife is a women's liberationist struggling to get out.

Then there are the linked or *Siamese hypochondriacs,* the mutual martyrs. The couple, usually of much character and bristly temperaments, who battle through a stormy marriage for most of their years. One of them has always been the hypochondriac and the other has been the barely tolerant complainer. But in the end the complainer develops self-protective symptoms and is brave about them (not too brave; just brave enough to leave the hypochondriacal partner well aware that he too—usually the he—has his troubles and is putting up with them manfully). Misgivings begin to overtake the original hypochondriac, and then kindness. Now she becomes as protective of his symptoms as of her own. And they totter down the twilight years happy in their mutual protection. They would love to go to the theater, but—they will have to call off the dinner because he, poor man, she, poor old girl, is not up to it. It is an odd but frequent method of impersonating Darby and Joan. I recall such a couple, now very aged, and living in perfect serenity. The husband explained to me some time ago: "I remember in the tough times, we were tempted to try psychoanalysis. Happily, we didn't do it. Our neuroses have grown together. Uproot one, and the whole tree would collapse."

Throughout all this, I have been going on an assumption we are all too unwilling to question. Which is that the hypochondriac is always unhappy. Let us end by considering the *happy hypochondriac,* of whom I humbly take myself to be one (until the next twinge of the diverticula, the sudden suspicion that somebody has just shot an arrow into the gluteus maximus). I sometimes think that the difference between an unhappy hypochondriac and a happy one is no more, but no less, than the difference between an unsuccessful and a successful show-off. Anxiety, I believe, is the secret spring of more things than bigotry, rudeness, conceit, and wit. I suggest that hypochondriasis is a special sort of failure to liberate anxiety. (And I am aware that to accept this theory, we shall have to give the lie to Gillespie's contention that anxiety has nothing to do with it.)

The anxious one yearns for the limelight but feels guilty about grabbing it (hence the saying that shyness is the most flagrant form of conceit). So the punishment takes the form of inducing pain to encourage the concern of friends and, above all, of the one person actually in control of the spotlight, the doctor. Among my hypochondriacal friends (you will have gathered by now, my many hypochondriacal friends) I count a formerly beautiful woman whose number of alarming symptoms has increased in direct proportion to the decline of her beauty. She has learned with Walter De la Mare, what is always heartbreakingly hard to accept, that "beauty vanishes, beauty passes, however rare, rare it be." I hope very much that her doctor exercises all the compassion of which he is capable, for while it is an ordeal in itself to be a woman, it is a difficult thing indeed to be a beauty from the start, and a handicap no one should be saddled with, and it becomes crueler and crueler as the spotlight veers away and leaves her in the unnoticed shade.

Women and beauty apart, I hope you will be sympathetic to this view of any hypochondriac as an anxious person who has not the luck, or the talent, to take the limelight by any other means than the eruption of symptoms.

But let us finally look at the happy hypochondriac, fortunate in talent, or beauty, or sheer gall. I am thinking not of the showoff merely, the social nuisance, the club bore, the Lady Bountiful. For the perfect example of what I have in mind, may I recall the peerless figure of Walter Hagen. For the laymen, may I quickly say that Walter Hagen, though not the greatest golfer who ever lived, was far and away the most colorful, the most outrageously unabashed, a master gamesman who made a habit of unnerving and beating better players through most of his prime. He dressed like a peacock and lived like a maharajah, at a time (in the early twenties) when professional golfers were meant to imitate their betters, and dress soberly, and say "sir." He introduced to England the two-tone footwear that became known as the "co-respondent's shoes." This bit of bounderism produced such a trauma in his British opponents that—according to Stephen Potter—it marked the end of the British dominance of the game.

Hagen decided that a pro was just as good as an amateur. And when he first encountered the English golf tradition whereby the members dined in the clubhouse, whereas the pros took their vittles belowstairs somewhere, Hagen simply hired a Rolls and a chauffeur and a butler, and a lunch prepared by the Savoy, arrived at the famous course, had the car drawn up in front of the clubhouse, ordered the butler to lay a tablecloth on the grass, and sat there quietly wolfing mousseline of salmon and cold turkey and champagne while the members seethed inside over their beer and sausage-and-mash. Never again was a professional refused the run of the clubhouse in British tournaments.

Hagen used to arrive on the first tee of a major championship, swing his club a couple of times, and drawl, "Waal, who's gonna be second?" He made a point of staying up drinking hideously late on the eve of a crucial match, and when his drooping friends came to to remind him that his archrival had been in bed for hours, he said, "He may be in bed, but he's not asleep." In a fine demonstration of the happy hypochondriac, he was once about to have his photograph taken with the other members of the Ryder Cup teams. They began to assemble out by the putting green, and Hagen was there early. This, he thought, was an error. He quietly slipped away to the clubhouse, sat down, and started up a cozy conversation with a friend. Half an hour later, the lawn was agog with cries of "Hagen! Find Hagen! Where's Hagen?" In the meantime, he had changed into a more resplendent outfit still, and at the last moment, when he had been given up, he ambled out to a chorus of "Ah, there he is, good old Walter."

Obviously, here a great deal of anxiety had to be placated. It was simply the luck of his temperament—that unanalyzed word again—that made him able to impose his hypochondriasis on everybody else and make it a joy instead of a bore. If the connection is unclear between this happy exhibitionism and the anxiety it liberated, may I just add that when he had gone past his prime, he retired to a small Pennsylvania town, among people who had never heard of him, went, you might say, into retreat; and for most of his later years was an invalid.

So, I can only say, after an experience of hypochondriasis which is getting to be rather long, that there are people of all ages, and of all sexes (male, female, and reconstructed), people plainly or dubiously hypochondriacal, who nevertheless need doctors. Not merely to tell them that the symptoms presage nothing serious, that nothing is the matter; but, whether or not anything is the matter, to tell them that they should do certain things under medical instruction—cut out the coffee, avoid pepper, take off the back brace and then put it back on again. I'm sure that most doctors long ago found out that reassurance is not always enough. The practiced hypochondriac is artful at inviting reassurance in order to reject it. And then the doctor himself, if he's not careful, is hurt and he, too, becomes a hypochondriac, though a licensed one. I am sure that what is needed is constant, patient instruction, the prescribing of innumerable placebos hailed as possible sovereign remedies. But at all times prescribed with compassion. For the doctor facing the hypochondriac is an essential substitute, in an irreligious age, for that Someone who is supposed to watch over us.

Finally, I return to the book which Dr. Robert Woods Brown and I have been brooding over, both in the surgery and on the fairways. We hope to keep it to under ten volumes. The title is mine, but the splendid subtitle is his. We hope to call it *The Hypochondriac's Handbook, or How to Scare the Daylights Out of Your Doctor and Still Retain the Affection of Your Loved Ones.**

*I feel bound to enrich further the literature of hypochondriasis by noting the emergence of a new breed: the *meticulous hypochondriac,* a category inspired by the scrupulous decision of a young, newly married California couple who, in 1985, resolved not to have a baby until they were sure that neither of them harbored a genetic disorder. Although they admitted to having no pathological suspicions about their respective families, they were told to track down the birth and death dates and the medical histories of each parent, aunt, uncle, brother, and sister; and then to subject themselves, through the good offices of a genetic foundation, to tests for each of the two thousand known genetic diseases. Presumably, the race is on between the testing and the menopause.

How It All Began

GIVEN BEFORE THE U.S. HOUSE OF REPRESENTATIVES,
WASHINGTON, D.C., SEPTEMBER 25, 1974, IN
COMMEMORATION OF THE 200TH ANNIVERSARY OF THE
FIRST CONTINENTAL CONGRESS

How It All Began

M r. Speaker, Mr. McDade, Members of the House, distinguished guests, ladies and gentlemen: Of all the times that I have sat in this House in the past thirty-odd years as a reporter and listened to presidents requesting from you declarations of war—not many of them anymore, since (according to the White House!) you lost the power!—listening to pronouncements that the State of the Union was good, bad, or indifferent, and listening to debates on everything from the price of battleships to the coloring of margarine, I can assure you that this occasion is for me far and away the most terrifying. It was not at first put up to me as an ordeal, or even as a very great privilege, which indeed it is. I understood that there was to be a cozy get-together of some Congressmen somewhere—a breakfast perhaps, at which I might be called on to say a few impromptu words. But standing here now, I feel as if I were just coming awake from a nightmare in which I saw myself before you unprepared and naked (as one often is in dreams) looking around this awesome assembly and blurting out: "I accept your nomination for the Presidency of the United States!"

When I blithely accepted—the invitation, that is—and the grandeur of this occasion was only then made clear to me, I tried to backtrack on the ground of a conflict of interest. Because

I was supposed now to be standing before an audience not in the United States but in the Kingdom of Fife, in Scotland, addressing the annual dinner of the Royal and Ancient Golf Club of St. Andrews. My letter of abject apology to the secretary prompted from him a chivalrous reply: "It is a pity," he wrote, "that you will not be following in the footsteps of Francis Ouimet and Robert Tyre Jones, Jr. But it is splendid that you should be following in the footsteps of Lafayette and Churchill." He added, however: "A senior member asks me to remind you that we are twenty years more ancient than the first Continental Congress, and maybe you should get your priorities straight."

I cannot help recalling, and with some pride in the great honor that you do me today, that the only native-born Englishman I ever heard address this House was Winston Churchill. He remarked then that if his father had been American and his mother English, instead of the other way round, "I might have got here on my own." The wistful thought occurs to me today that if *my* father had been Irish, and my mother English, instead of the other way round, I might have tiptoed, at a respectful distance, in the shadow of that mighty man.

We are met in what I take to be the first official celebration of the Bicentennial by the Congress to applaud the men who met in Philadelphia in September 1774, in response to many indignities, mainly, I think, to the military occupation of Boston and the monstrous, and as it turned out the fateful, blunder of the Parliament in closing the port of Boston. This was an action which Englishmen, to this day, might think of as being not particularly unreasonable, until you ask them how they would feel if the Congress of the United States were to close the port of London.

Those first Congressmen were a very mixed bunch of aggrieved men, though we tend to see them as a body of blue-eyed, selfless patriots all at one in their detestation of tyranny. But I doubt that the present Congress spans so wide a political gamut. They ranged from hidebound radicals to bloodshot conservatives. There were, of course, many disinterested men fighting for a principle, but there were also shrewd businessmen who saw, in a possible break with England, a gorgeous opportunity to ally with Spain and control all trade east as well as west of the Appalachians.

But—and it will be worth saying over and over in the next two years—the lovers of liberty carry no national passport. And this seems to me a good time to recall some unsung heroes of the American Revolution who sat not in Philadelphia but in the House of Commons, some of them who jeopardized their careers by taking the colonists' side. Henry Seymour Conway, who carried through the repeal of the Stamp Act. General John Burgoyne, himself to be the invasion commander, who raised a storm by urging Parliament to convince the colonies "by persuasion and not by the sword." Captain George Johnstone, of the Royal Navy and once the governor of Florida, who warned the House of Commons that what it was doing would provoke a confederacy and a general revolt—a flash of foresight that made the government benches rise and tell him he had "brought his knowledge of America to the wrong market." Most of all, there was Edmund Burke, who got a respectful hearing on anything and everything until he rose to refute the argument that if the citizens of Boston were taxed without representation, they were no worse off than the citizens of Manchester. Burke replied: "So, then, because some towns in England are not represented, America is to have no representative at all? They are our children [and] when they wish to reflect the best face of the parent, the countenance of British liberty, are we to turn to them the shameful parts of our Constitution?" He was booed to the rafters.

By recalling these transatlantic heroes of the Revolution, I wish only to suggest the dangers that lie ahead, and that have lain in the past, in our tendency, especially in the movies and television, and in too many schoolbooks, to sentimentalize our history or to teach it as a continual clash between the good guys and the bad guys, between America and Britain, the white man and the Indian, industry and labor—between us and them.

Practical men distrust history as a false guide (Henry Ford said it was "the bunk"), and they are right if they mean simply that nothing ever repeats itself in the same way. It is rather the tendency of history to repeat itself in every way but one, and the new element is unfortunately usually the only one that matters. So it is a normal impulse in men of action—and I take it that I am looking at men who are nothing but men of action—to distrust history because it is done with. Americans are all activists in the sense that they have always believed that tomorrow is going to be at least as good as today and certainly better than yesterday. Nothing could be more American than the famous remark of Lincoln Steffens after he visited the Soviet Union: "I have seen the future, and it works!" Bertrand Russell saw the same future at the same time, and what he saw was the past in a new guise, and it chilled his blood. But then, Russell had a passion for human liberty, and he could smell tyranny even when he couldn't see it. Steffens, on the other hand, though in earlier years a penetrating and compassionate muckraker, evolved in Russia into a type of reporter not yet extinct: a reporter who believed everything he was told.

We are about to launch ourselves on a two-year festival of commemoration of the American past. From the early promises of some chambers of commerce, television producers, motel proprietors, and manufacturers of buttons and medals, it could turn into an orgy of self-righteousness. Practically every man who signed the Declaration of Independence is at this moment being measured for a halo or, at worst, a T-shirt. This is done, I think, from a fear that the truth might turn out to be dull. Well, it's often embarrassing, but it's never dull. By sentimentalizing our history we do, most of all, an enormous disservice to the young. We imply, or proclaim, that the United States was invented by saints with a grievance. Now, any perceptive twelve-year-old knows from his experience of life that this is nonsense—and any perceptive five-year-old from *her* experience of life. So they transfer their healthy suspicions from the teacher to what is being taught and conclude that American history is a great bore.

Professor Jensen has reminded us that we have the word of a man who was in the thick of things from the start—John Adams—that in 1776 no more than a third of the population was on the revolutionary side. One third was openly or covertly Loyalist. And the other third was that dependable minority to whom the Gallup Poll pays regular tribute: the people who "don't know," don't feel anything, don't stand for anything.

We are also undoubtedly going to be plunged, through the TV tube, into a public bath of immigrants, all of whom will be warm-hearted, simple, courageous, and abused. But it would do no harm to young Americans—it ought rather to fortify their ideals—to learn that many a shipload of immigrants from 1848 into our own time contained also men jumping military service, and delinquents both juvenile and adult: a lot of people with a lot to hide. This does not demean, indeed to me it glorifies, the legions who struggled for a decent and a tidy life. To know this will only confirm the daily experience of young people growing up today in a community of mixed national and racial origins. By such teaching of the truth—of *the way it was*—in all its maddening complexity, they might learn early on the simple lesson that courage and cowardice know no national or racial frontiers, and that when we say a man or woman is a credit to the race, we should mean no more or less than the human race. The war against injustice and bigotry and greed started well before 1774 (in fact, with Cain and Abel) and will trouble our history till the end of time.

Now, I think it is good and proper that in 1976 we should

celebrate what is best in the American past. But we should remember that our history, like that of all nations, is sometimes fine and sometimes foul. The important thing is to know which is which. For if we accept at any given time the inevitable complexity of human motives and desires that make up the past and the present, there is no need to fear. But, some people say, won't a strong dose of reality destroy the idealism of the young? It is the same question that a member of the Constitutional Convention put to James Madison when he said that good government must be based on "ambition counteracting ambition." Was he saying, asked a mocking delegate, that "the frailties of human nature are the proper elements of good government"? Madison replied: "I know no other." That simple sentence, which reflects Madison's unsleeping sense of reality, and his ability to set up a system that hopes for the best in human nature but is always on guard against the worst—that is what, I believe, has guaranteed the survival of the Constitution as a hardy and practical instrument of government.

So I suggest that we would be making a foolish spectacle of ourselves if we spent the Bicentennial year proclaiming to a bored world that we are unique and holier than anybody. For today, national sovereignty is a frail commodity. Today, we and Western Europe are faced with a triple threat to representative government. For the first time since the fifteenth century, our cities are threatened by the success of violence. For the first time since the 1920s, our countries are threatened by an unstoppable inflation. And for the first time in human history, our planet is threatened by an unstopped nuclear arms race. We are very much in the parlous situation of the thirteen colonies. We don't have much time left to go on thinking of ourselves as separate nations whose fate is in our own hands. Franklin's warning is apt: "We must all hang together, or assuredly we shall all hang separately." More and more we, and many other nations, are—as the Bible warned us—"members one of another."

I think that honest persons who are concerned for the reputation of this country abroad had much cause for misgiving in the past year or two, when our image was rendered alarming to free men by the gradual growth in the executive branch of government (it began a dozen or fourteen years ago) of a kind of domestic Politburo which, in the end, in its malignant form, was indifferent to the Congress and contemptuous of the people and the law. But then, through the gloom and squalor that lay on this city, there came a strong beam of light, and it came from this House. Nothing that I can remember has redeemed, in Europe anyway, the best picture of America—which is always the one that ordinary men and women *want* to believe in—more than the recent public sessions (and how fortunate that they were public) of your Judiciary Committee.* Here, after a welter of truth, and possible truth, and rumor and hearsay, we saw and heard thirty-eight men and women debating with sense and dignity and seriousness the most dire threat to the Constitutional system since 1860. And so long as the standing committees of Congress remember that they are standing in for nobody but the people, the state of the Constitution will be sound. And just so long will the executive be "the servant not the proprietor of the people."

So it seems to me a happy thing, and enough of a celebration for today, at any rate, that two hundred years after the first Congress met as a team of watchdogs eager to corner a tyrannical executive, this House should have made it possible for us today to say without complacency, and with some legitimate pride, "I have seen the past—and it works!"

---

*This was the committee that resolved the Watergate scandal by voting to impeach President Nixon, who thereupon resigned the Presidency on August 9, 1974, seven weeks before this speech was given.

Shakespeare in America

GIVEN BEFORE THE FIRST WORLD SHAKESPEARE
CONGRESS, IN WASHINGTON, D.C., APRIL 19, 1976

Shakespeare in America

It would be easy, and it would seem to be no more than a courtesy, in addressing a conference that has chosen the title "Shakespeare in America," to follow those works of American scholarship which ardently examine Shakespeare's view of the relations between the individual and the state and end in the discovery that he would have been either a Republican or a Democrat. If this sounds naive, it is not more naive than the continuing scholarly efforts to prove that on the contrary he was a lawyer, an atheist, a doctor, a spiritualist, a Christian Scientist, or a Marxist. The noblest of these attempts to show that Shakespeare was spiritually itching to be an American is that of the late Charles Mills Gayley. Alas, Professor Gayley was writing in 1917 during the First War, and he came to the triumphant conclusion that Shakespeare would have been solidly on the Allied side.

In a Bicentennial year, it is a natural folly to see all our heroes in retrospect as inevitable supporters of the American Revolution. But I hope you will be relieved to hear that I am not going to shuffle through those monographs—about what Shakespeare meant, say, to the English settlers of America—which also tend to come to the thoughtful conclusion that if Shakespeare had been born a hundred and fifty years later, he would certainly have emigrated to America and probably have beaten Thomas Jefferson to the writing of the Declaration of Independence. On the contrary, I imagine that if Shakespeare had been in America, and in his prime in 1783 or thereabouts, we might have had from him a play of such amused contempt for the sunshine patriots, such compassion for the persecution of the Loyalists, and such eloquent but mixed admiration for the Founding Fathers themselves that—in the first hot flashes of their change of life—they might well have forced him to seek a haven in Canada or the West Indies, or even back in that England in which, as one sad soldier wrote, "there will scarcely be a village without some American dust in it by the time we are all at rest."

But if we are to take a brief retrospective look at Shakespeare in America, you will be happy to hear that we hardly need to begin much before the 1830s. There is no need at all to wonder what the Founders of New England thought about Shakespeare. They didn't. In all the colonial literature of the seventeenth century there is, I believe, hardly an allusion to him. Harvard College showed its usual enlightenment by acquiring its first copy of Shakespeare in 1723, eighty-seven years after its founding. And even forty or fifty years later, while the Founding Fathers of the Republic were thoroughly at home with Rousseau and Montesquieu and Voltaire, it is safe to guess that few if any of them were acquainted with Shakespeare. Jefferson, who was known as a prodigy for the eclecticism of his reading, mentions Shakespeare three times.

In such learned company as this, I had better throw it out as a suggestion rather than a thesis that New England as a Shakespearean desert may well be explained by the Puritans' intense obsession with theological literature, by their moral authoritarianism, which banished plays and players as summarily as Cromwell had done. As late as 1686, Cotton Mather was alarmed by what he called "much discourse of beginning stage plays," at a time when playhouses were scattered through the colonies from New York to Charleston—but not in New England, and not playing Shakespeare. And the dearth of Shakespearean productions after the Revolution may be charitably put down to the prevailing chauvinism, the determination of the new Americans to write their own plays and music and abjure, in particular, the works of the defeated enemy.

It took, indeed, about sixty years for the Republic to welcome Shakespearean productions, and not until the mid-nineteenth century did it spawn its first native Shakespearean actor (the son of an immigrant London actor) in Edwin Booth. Even then, Mrs. Trollope was shocked to find that in the more civilized cities, Shakespeare was thought to be obscene; which is not surprising now when you consider that for the thirty years or so before the Civil War, literate Americans were brought up on Noah Webster's authorized version of the Bible, in which "to go a-whoring" was replaced by "go astray," "breast" was substituted for "teat," and "cone" for "nipple."

It comes, then, as a surprise—to me, at any rate—to find that the first *popularization* of Shakespeare happened far from the Eastern cities or seats of learning. It came from strolling players who followed the flatboats floating down the Allegheny and rode into the rowdier pioneer towns springing up around and across the Appalachians. Actors were generally regarded as vagabonds, chronic debtors, and sexual fly-by-nights. And the expanding frontier was a wonderful wide place to perform in, pick up the box-office receipts, and get lost, before descending on another settlement that could be counted on to be gullible— for one night only.

But where did these vagabonds get their knowledge of Shakespeare, and how could the frontier settlements know a little about him and want to know more? Well, it is a pleasure for me, among such a frightening body of *savants,* to point to a name that I doubt has ever been mentioned in scholarly circles.

It is that of William Holmes McGuffey, the son of Scotch-Irish parents who moved into western Pennsylvania in the immediate wake of the defeated Indians. The family went on into what the noted encyclopedia published in Chicago calls "the primeval forests of Ohio." There McGuffey became a teacher in the rural schools at the age of thirteen, picked up private tuition here and there, and at twenty-five was an instructor in ancient languages. But his passion was for grounding the frontier children in the best models of their own language. In 1835 he put out two school readers, and they were bought in job lots and used as basic English textbooks in the very elementary schools of the empire of the Mississippi and the South. In the sixth edition there were 138 selections from over a hundred authors, and Shakespeare was the preferred author of choice, with nine extracts. Time and again the memoirs of pioneers across three thousand miles are studded with saws and instances from the Bible, *Pilgrim's Progress,* and Shakespeare. Children in log huts who could only imagine New York or London, and who, unlike the divines of New England, had never heard of Rousseau or Goethe, could—unlike the divines of New England—yet quote Hamlet and recite the Fall of Wolsey. For the distribution of the McGuffey readers stopped short of New England. Everywhere else, the readers sold, at last count, something like two hundred million copies.

It is too much to believe that while Boston and Philadelphia were honoring Shakespeare in the breach, the Republic's literate reputation was redeemed by such genteel, florid scoundrels as the type of W. C. Fields, always one step ahead of the bailiffs. But these early roving actor-managers discovered two things: that their audiences on the rivers and the prairie wanted to know where Wolsey had fallen from, and why Henry V got so excited at Agincourt. They also found that once Shakespeare had been dinned into simple folk as the grandest figure of the literary

Establishment, he was—like other grandees of the Establishment—fair game for burlesque.

I hope it does not pain any patriot present to know that
within fifty years of the founding of the Republic, the revolutionary heroes too were quickly stripped of their haloes and
became, on the frontier, comic characters. And so with Shakespeare's magnificoes. The frontier appetite for blood and thunder
matched that of the Elizabethans themselves. After all, stabbings
and gunfights were fairly common in the experience of the audience. And what these tough audiences wanted were murders
and ghosts and sleepwalkings, and a noisy suffocation of Des-
demona. The comedies were very rarely played, because the
playing of the tragedies was comedy enough. In a performance
of *Hamlet* in Pittsburgh, a city said at the time to be "sunk in
sin and coal," the actor playing the gravedigger saw the bailiffs
in the wings and hopped into the grave, beat it through the trap
door, and was never seen again. A popular performance of *O-
thello* ended with the Moor rolling in agony over the stage apron
so that he could pick up a fiddle and play his own funeral march.
For a couple of decades such theater as could be called legitimate
came to a stop and was overtaken by burlesque. Byron's *Manfred*
was played in blackface, and a moving chorus of "Nearer My
God to Thee" was interpolated in the third act of *Faust*.

Oddly enough, the only serious plays to which the frontier
audiences came to pay an almost ritual respect were ones glo-
rifying the American Indian. In Florida in the 1830s a company
took the risk of putting on a Shakespearean performance during
the second Seminole War. The entire company was butchered
by the Indians, who looted the costume trunks and galloped off
dressed as Orlando, Macbeth, and Othello. But once the Indian
had been pushed out of the Mississippi Valley and driven west,
he—who was not acceptable as a neighbor—became admirable
as a tragic hero. Far more than any Shakespearean character,

he was applauded and wept over, by the people who had hounded him, as a noble and cheated figure.

But in the great age of burlesque, the Indian was represented as a character equally as comic as the conquering white. In the parodies of the sentimental Indian melodrama, the vehicle of parody is Shakespearean. There is one that contrives a witty switch on a mixed marriage. It is about the hoariest of American legends, that about Captain Smith confronting the Indian chief Powhatan to be saved by his beautiful daughter, though Smith makes pretty clear that that was not his prime purpose in crossing the Atlantic. He begins:

> Most potent, grave and reverend fellow—
> To use the words of that black Othello—
> My very noble and approved good savage,
> That we came out here your lands to ravage
> Is most true; for this you see us banded.

Powhatan says:

> Pray, sir, how do you mean to set about it?

Smith:

> Easy enough; we have full powers to treat.

Powhatan:

> If that's the case, I'll take some whiskey neat.

Throughout the nineteenth century this theatrical impudence never flagged. In the mining towns of Colorado and California, Macbeth disposed of Duncan with a six-shooter, and the celebrated Emma Abbott soliloquized as Juliet, on a trapeze.

If this spirit is a wounding thing to academics, it is what made life bearable among the peoples who tried to knot a social lifeline across the wilderness. It is that saving sort of American humor which reaches from these rivermen and players through Mark Twain to the Marx Brothers and Woody Allen: the humor of the skeptical or soured immigrant. When the frontier was officially pronounced closed in 1890, an anonymous poet wrote its epitaph:

Across the plains where once there roamed the Indian and the
    scout,
The Swede with alcoholic breath sets rows of cabbage out.

By then there were enough established cities ready for the real thing: for the full-fledged Shakespearean performance.

But if we now look back with condescending tolerance on the audacities of these frontier folk, I don't think we should deceive ourselves that modern audiences, either in America or Britain, are that much more sensitive to the depth and subtlety of Shakespeare's language. It is why we need to study it all the time, with all the resources of rational scholarship and responsive feeling. For I suspect that for most of the audiences today as yesterday, his language is a kind of rich Muzak against which— as Fritz Kreisler said about his violin music—the audience sits back and indulges its fantasies. Certainly, I have sat through many performances in this country in which, for instance, Mercutio's raw vulgarity at the expense of the Nurse provoked not a wince in the audience. I have yet to hear a ripple of recognition for the definitive account of the three most potent effects of alcohol on man as given by that veteran alcoholic, the Porter in *Macbeth*. And when it comes to such dense and brilliant syntax as that in Hamlet's lesser-known soliloquies, or in the special pleading of Iachimo, one is bound to feel that a modern audience has only the faintest idea what even the argument is all about.

The stock answer to this rather haughty complaint, which implies that whoever else Shakespeare is for he is not for children, is that even barely understood music is good for the soul, that children are like the French beans in Charles Darwin's famous experiment: if you play a trombone at them, something is bound to happen.

I have said enough, I hope, to show that Shakespeare has had, for more than a century at any rate, a lively and peculiar life in America, apart from his industrial usefulness in the manufacturing of graduate theses. This conference is an international one, and even in this festival political year it is surely not our business to vindicate the ways of Shakespeare to the Constitution of the United States, or to any other ideology. For if Shakespeare had not transcended all ideologies, he would not be the universal man we meet here to honor. Sooner or later, students, theatergoers, scholars, all of us have to say why he is unique and why— through all the tidal waves of fashion down four centuries—he still rides the crest.

I shall end, then, by trying to distinguish two types of genius.

I don't know if it is an act of legitimate criticism or a wistful exercise in wishful thinking to see in the most universal artists a temperament of great sweetness allied to an unflinching perception of the human condition. The men I have in mind are Chaucer, Michelangelo, Mozart, and Shakespeare.

Below them is a small flock of more positive, and possibly braver, characters whose genius lies in the honesty of their striving for the sublime tolerance that the greater ones appear to have at birth. I am thinking now of Goethe, Wagner, Tolstoy, Mark Twain.

Well below them are all the rest of us, who oscillate between acceptance and protest and fall short of wisdom precisely to the extent that we see only part of the nature of men and women or rail at it.

I doubt that there has been in our time a wiser distinction made between artists of the first rank than that which Sir Isaiah Berlin picked up and elaborated from a line of the Greek poet Archilochus: "The fox knows many things, but the hedgehog knows one big thing." Taken figuratively, says Berlin, "these words can be made to yield a sense in which they mark one of the deepest differences which divide writers and thinkers, and it may be, human beings in general. For there exists a great chasm between those, on the one side, who relate everything to a single central vision . . . and, on the other side, those who pursue many ends, often unrelated and even contradictory . . . seizing upon a vast variety of experiences and objects for what they are in themselves without, consciously or unconsciously, seeking to fit them into . . . a unitary vision."

Berlin gives as supreme examples of the hedgehog: Plato, Dante, and Dostoevski. And of the fox: Aristotle, Shakespeare, and Pushkin. This thesis has the advantage, over my rather more desperate one, of making no judgment of value. It does not praise Molière at the expense of Ibsen, or Shakespeare at the expense of Dostoevski. It says: here are two types of genius, two fundamentally distinct, if not opposed, views of life. Bearing in mind the remarkable researches in our time into molecular biology, I should prefer to say that it distinguishes not so much between two views of life (since it is possible to *adopt* a view of life that may not fit one's character): it distinguishes between two temperaments radically differentiated at birth—perhaps by no more than an inherited disposition of chromosomes. However it comes about, the distinction is true and binding. It is not possible to mistake *Don Giovanni* for a work of the *Ring* cycle. No one has ever thought that *Le Bourgeois Gentilhomme* was written by Ibsen. Or that Bernard Shaw wrote *The Tempest*.

Artists apart, I do believe that all of us fall into one or the other category. Rarely in social life does the difference appear sharper than between two people of not necessarily different political views but different political temperaments. There is the idealist—the hedgehog—who, often nobly, wants to set things right. He is always in danger of corruption from the Peer Gynt syndrome, the impulse to break everybody in sight on the wheel of his precious "integrity." There is the realist, so called—the fox—who sees, or pretends to see, more clearly the complexities and contradictions of the political situation. Shakespeare registers the force of both impulses, and records what the life of the politician so often reflects—the natural tragedy of their failure to reconcile their ideals in useful action.

Nowhere does he illumine this sense of political realism better than in *Coriolanus*. And nothing could be more Shakespearean than the fact that the best critics—from Coleridge to Dowden—have argued whether *Coriolanus* is a political play at all. Stopford Brooke was convinced that Shakespeare sided with the people, Hazlitt that he was prejudiced in favor of the patricians.

This conflict between the two types has, so far as I know, never been more consciously or confidently provoked than in the armed assault of Bernard Shaw, alive, on Shakespeare, dead. For much of the fire that fueled Shaw's famous campaign sprang from his exasperated envy of a playwright who successfully plumbed the depths of human goodness and evil, reason and instinct, common sense and idiosyncrasy, without once wishing to enlist his insight in the service of a cause, a crusade, a religion, or a nonreligion. Shaw could not bear the thought that Shakespeare knew better than Shaw the damaging power of sexual passion and yet gave no hint that Cleopatra ought to be taken out and scrubbed and compelled to become a lieutenant in the army of General Christabel Pankhurst.

This is the anger of the crusader against the man of the world. It is the contempt of the evangelist for the reporter. And that brings us to what I hope is the relevance of Shakespeare to us, considered as involuntary victims of the media, in the twilight of the twentieth century. Simply, if you can bear the humble word, that Shakespeare is the greatest reporter we have had in English.

I speak feelingly about this, because most of my life I have been a reporter, embracing in public no political party, supporting no faction, on the principle that a reporter must try to represent, as fairly yet as vividly as possible, the flux of argument and emotion mobilized to defeat the complexity of the facts of life around him. It is the stance of the fox. (He is, by the way, not to be confused with the dedicated "investigative" reporter, who is a hedgehog in fox's clothing.)

This definition makes the reporter sound very high-minded indeed. But no ordinarily honest man can escape the suspicion that it is, in some societies, a very tactful position to adopt. Looking on from above the battle, and reporting it as disinterestedly as one can, very easily coincides with the safe position of sitting on the fence and with the daily practice of that "craven scruple/Of thinking too precisely on th' event,/A thought which, quarter'd, hath but one part wisdom/And ever three parts coward." And all reporters should be warned by that remark which Lloyd George made about a cabinet minister who prided himself on his sense of fairness and balance: "He sat on the fence so long that the iron entered into his soul."

As a citizen, one must commit oneself. One must vote. As a reporter, one must strive to recognize that, in a clash of political factions on even the weightiest issues, the antagonists are equally endowed—if not with wisdom—with the follies and frailties of human nature.

It is inevitable that the hedgehogs should despise this stance as one of prudence at best, and Shakespeare's serenity as nothing better than surrender. Hence the blazing Shavian sentence (all the more pointed, in that it was not written by him but by his most brilliant parodist): "Shakespeare had glimpses of the havoc of displacement wrought by Elizabethan romanticism in the

social machine . . . [but in the end] he consoled himself by offering the world a soothing doctrine of despair." I hope we are
all here to say—as incurable foxes—not so.

So I end on hailing him as the king of the foxes. It may
be said that he remains the supreme expression, in the English
language, of the human spirit—but only if we are prepared to
define that resounding platitude. I can define crudely its most
elementary exercise as the inextinguishable urge of one human
being *to say freely* what happened to him, what he feels, and
what is on his mind, and by so doing strike a spark of grateful
recognition in another human being. The essential condition is
"to say freely." And it is an instinct more and more liable to
suppression since the most frightening political phenomenon of
our time is the general contraction or abolition of free societies.

I don't know if there are nations that ban Shakespeare on
ideological grounds. I am told that among what we sheepishly
call closed societies—that is to say, among tyrannies—it is
thought better simply to ignore him. If so, an ideologue of our
day may say that it was only Shakespeare's cunning talent as a
fox that saved him from the Tower of London. For there is
always something in Shakespeare that can be used, or manip-
ulated, to bolster any political position, any religious or skeptical
view of life. I would rather say that it is the universality of his
sympathy for all the expressions of the human spirit, benevolent
or malign, committed or neutral, that makes him, three hundred
and sixty years after his death, the archetype of the literary genius
as a free man, and makes even tyrants pay him the skulking
tribute of neglect.

Staying Alive in 1776

GIVEN BEFORE THE COLLEGE OF PHYSICIANS OF
PHILADELPHIA, JULY 8, 1976

Staying Alive in 1776

Much of the anniversary prose that resounds throughout the Republic in an anniversary year—in print or over the
tube, and surely in commencement addresses—is inevitably devoted to fattening the romantic myths on which patriotism feeds.
But the urge to debunk is equally a form of dogmatism. And if
the aim of this lecture were simply to puncture the myths, we
would be left with a picture not much closer to real life but
with a vacuum inhabited by lifeless puppets. My aim is no more,
but no less, than what I take to be at all times the first concern
of the historian: to try and revive the actual life of a time, to
say as clearly as possible the way things probably were.

So I want this evening to attempt to compose a picture of
health and disease as they were experienced, and regarded by
most people, by the doctors and the laymen, two hundred years
ago, in this part of the country especially. I leave it to others to
recall a neglected, or unread, chapter in the history of this nation,
namely the medical practice of the Indian tribes, and the healing
arts of the missionary priests like Father Junípero Serra who
were busy, at exactly the same time, civilizing or—whether they
wanted it or not—Christianizing the natives of the Pacific Coast.

In October of 1775, there arrived in New York a doctor
famous throughout New England, a man who had acquired a

specially glowing reputation among the people of Boston. He was a Dr. Dubuque. And he was a quack. If it seems unjust to begin with him, may I remind you that—apart from the appearance of a giant or two, like Hunter, Morgagni, or Jenner—the eighteenth century was a comparatively uncreative time in the history of medicine, and it has been well said by Sir William Ogilvie that in the eighteenth century, "quacks flourished as never before or since."

At any rate, Dr. Dubuque offered, in handbills and newspaper advertisements, to cure "green wounds, black jaundice, the bloody flux, hare lip, and venereal disease." The New Englanders of those days, not having at their elbow the protective wisdom of the *New England Journal of Medicine,* were evidently more gullible than the New Yorkers. Within six months of his arrival in New York, a pretext was found to get rid of Dr. Dubuque: He was charged with stealing indigo and was convicted. He was branded, literally, and he vanished.

To us, 1775 may seem awfully late for any quack to survive and prosper. The King's College Medical School had been founded eight years before. But before that, New York had no licensing system for doctors. There was no society of doctors or surgeons and no hospital. And throughout the century, in New York and most other places, there was nowhere for doctors officially to exchange their records or their experience. There was little disposition to do it, either, for—as somebody said—"each doctor feared a design to supplant him in his trade."

But by 1776, as you know, Philadelphia could boast of the first medical school in America, and the first real American hospital was already twenty-five years old. Yet everywhere else, "hospitals," so-called, were not generally looked on as progressive institutions. Most literate people shared the prejudice of the scholar who saw them as "places which rob the purse of the public in order to bolster up the lazy and the ignorant." What strikes me most forcibly about the medical picture of the eighteenth century, whether in Europe or in America, is the wide gap between the expertise (such as it was) of the doctors and the folklore of the laymen, however otherwise well educated. Medical histories tend to imply by omission that educated people were up on the current theory of acidosis, Cullen's classification of fevers, and Benjamin Rush's exciting doctrine of "excitability" as the cause of "irregular or convulsive" blood vessels. The histories I have read, at any rate, imply at the least that educated people were disposed to approve of these discoveries at a respectful distance, as marvels beyond them; as today, most of us laymen are obediently impressed by such mysteries as the structure of the DNA molecule or the Japanese work on transferred bacterial resistance. But most of the literate letters and journals in the eighteenth century appear, on the contrary, to suggest that doctors were regarded as necromancers rollicking in an indigenous jargon that had little to do with the actual healing of the sick. The enlightened eighteenth-century layman might have been just as impressed by the contemporary lingo of the trade as we are by the Greek and Latin polysyllables that doctors swap when they are together and with which, also, they intimidate skeptical or rebellious patients. But all this eighteenth-century talk of emaciation, swellings, fluxes, and discolorations, whereby doctors defined separate afflictions, did not give pause to the layman's rooted preference for classifying all illnesses by their symptoms, a preference which, I imagine, is still universal. He didn't care about the miasmic theory of disease, but he did know that dead animals and bad smells from a marsh carried trouble. Doctors at that time might divide between the two armies of the rationalists and the empiricists. But the layman was a thoroughgoing empiricist, even if he didn't know it. If he was ignorant, he was all for Dr. Dubuque and his miracle cures. If he was educated, he swore by the Dr. Spock of household medicine in those days: the surprising figure of John Wesley.

Wesley's handbook, *Primitive Physic,* went into many

editions in both England and America, and it confirmed the layman's distrust of general causes and his reliance on the pain he was feeling at the time. Wesley was, in fact, the prince of dogmatic empiricists. From his very wide observation on circuit he derived his dogma that such a medicine removes such a pain. And in proceeding from this hypothesis, he brilliantly reflected the educated prejudice against the whole medical profession. He condemned the best contemporary practice by saying that doctors were not content to note an illness and prescribe a cure but insisted on going into "causes," till at length, he wrote, "Physic becomes an abstruse science quite out of the reach of ordinary men." What surely is astonishing today is the presumption of an alert mind and a famous scholar that medicine properly belongs within the reach of the ordinary man. Wesley went on to denounce the fashion (I suppose *we* should say the notable advance) of compounding medicines, instead of trusting to God's provision of single healing plants. A prejudice that must have been appealing, by the way, to Philadelphians, and may have sparked their initiative in establishing the first medicinal herb garden in America.

Wesley's general prescription was simple: "Note the pain or the pustule. Go to the plant, thou sluggard." For measles, toast and water. For any cancer (meaning, then, any chancre or sore), hog's grease roasted in an apple. For "the small pox, resin shaken in water." Throughout all the dreadful epidemics of smallpox, this "tar-water" treatment, as it was called, was the sovereign remedy or, at least, the favorite prescription.

I imagine that in the eighteenth century, as in our own, at least half of a doctor's potential patients were hypochondriacs. But such was the general distrust of doctors that the anxious citizen did not so readily do what we do: dash off to a doctor at the first wince of a pinprick or a bellyache. He dashed off to Wesley's *Primitive Physic* and practiced self-medication. Doctors were notorious for weird and dangerous practices like bleeding and violent purging. Just because such assaults were done on George Washington and Alexander Hamilton was no reason for the ordinary citizen to subject himself to the leeches or the apothecary's fearsome brews. (For a time, by the way, the tar-water treatment for smallpox was as much of a controversy among the learned as are, today, Dr. Linus Pauling's claims for vitamin C.)

So if, in our day, the layman's road to Shangri-La is paved with vitamins, in the eighteenth century it was paved with the wonders of a naturalist's pharmacopoeia: with fox root, dried goat's blood, camphor oil, rhubarb, and henna. For the smart-aleck layman on to a good thing, magical cures (for what?) were reported from the broth of a stag's cooked penis. This was a favorite prescription in the South, but only, I suppose, because it was easier to come by in the Great Smokies than in Rittenhouse Square.

Thomas Jefferson, an inquisitive mole in the field of med-icine as in every other field, ardently recommended to the parents of sick children the wonderful properties of Seneca root, and at one time he urged the Secretary of War to substitute capsicum for the troops' ration of grog. "Capsicum," he enthused, "is indigenous to Texas and is a perennial there; and the pods and berries, when ground, provide a remarkable cure for disorders of the alimentary canal." Perhaps the colonial canal was tougher than ours. Luckily, in any case, the Secretary of War turned a deaf ear: capsicum is cayenne pepper, which I believe we should say is a marvelous *provoker* of disorders of the alimentary canal.

These, then, were the medical theories, the popular su-perstitions, and the general remedies of the time. (I suppose I ought to jog the memory of anyone who thinks these herbal remedies barbarous or new by noting that they had been stan-dard, and often effective, cures since the revered Galen in the second century A.D.; and that many of them are the root element of some of our most fashionable medications.) So, the main hazards to survival in the late eighteenth century were cholera and yellow fever, and smallpox (imported by Cortes in exchange for the export to Europe of syphilis). There was also—by our standards—an appalling rate of infant and toddler mortality. And everybody—man, woman, or child—was, of course, susceptible to most of our regular afflictions, then unrecognized as disease entities but lumped together, or described apart, by such imaginative names as I have mentioned; fluxes, wastings, and the like, including "fevers," which must have been a large, vague category, embracing in turn a great many diseases of mysterious etiology: for not for another hundred years was malaria connected with mosquitoes, and the baleful effects of microorganisms were unknown.

If you lived in remote settlements far from the East Coast, there was still the prospect of annihilation or maiming by Indians on sporadic raids. And if you lived in Philadelphia, you ran an abnormal risk of dysentery, thanks to the city's—even then—notoriously foul drinking water.

But once the war was on, there were two quite new threats to health and survival, the first being the special threats of a soldier's life. It may seem very late in this talk to unveil this glimpse of the obvious. I should guess that most people, being asked to name the commonest cause of death between 1776 and '83 (among the male population anyway), would immediately think of fatal battle wounds. On the contrary, the battle casualties were no more than two in a hundred: a pleasantly shocking statistic to us, who for a hundred years and more have been inured to the preconception of war as a collision between huge armies in set battles. (In the Second World War, the Russian soldier had only two chances in three of emerging unscathed.) But the Revolutionary War was fought in many places scattered over a vast terrain. A standing, or national, army was a novelty. It called on all trades and professions, and its recruits could choose their term of service—one month, six months, or as long as they cared to stay. Very few signed up for the duration, under the inspiration of Patrick Henry's quixotic demand "Give me liberty or give me death." (He, by the way, having once sounded his thrilling battle-cry, and arranged for the arming of the Virginia militia, became governor of the state, ordered an expedition into Illinois, and subsequently declined offers of serving as a delegate to Congress or to the Constitutional Convention, or as a United States Senator, or as Secretary of State, or as Chief Justice of the Supreme Court, or as envoy to France, and died in his bed at the age of sixty-three.)

The "embattled farmers" were remarkable for fighting only when their own acres were embattled. They practiced guerrilla warfare for a week or a weekend; and when the war, like a thunderstorm, moved on, they went back to their chores. How, then, to explain the very heavy mortality in the Continental Army? In a brilliant and exhaustive piece of research,* Virginia R. Allen has conclusively demonstrated that "nine American soldiers died from disease for every one killed by the British"; that "the odds of leaving a hospital alive were only seventy-five in a hundred"; that "during the summers of 1780 and 1781, Cornwallis's army in the Carolinas was so sick that large-scale action was impossible"; and that just about the worst fate that could befall an American soldier was to be captured and sent off to a British prison ship, where the sick and the well were packed in the airless holds, and were ill fed and abominably ill treated. They dropped like flies. According to the military journal of one James Thacher, on one ship fifteen hundred died in a few weeks.

The ordinary serving soldier, encamped in fields in all weathers, faced special hazards: heatstroke, frostbite, tetanus, malaria, and what they called "hospital sickness"—typhus. Since the country had always relied on local militias, there was no

*Oklahoma State Medical Association Journal, Sept.-Nov. 1970, Sept. 1971.

organized national military medical service. True, Congress had created a hospital department of the army in 1775, but it was so racked by political bickering and incompetence that it barely got going throughout the war, and the soldiers were very much at the mercy of any local healer calling himself a doctor.

In the war in the South, the British introduced what one British general called "a useful tactic of war." It was the cutting off of the enemy's water supply and the pollution of its wells, thereby assisting the likelihood of dysentery and typhoid. If you were in the navy, you ran the usual risk of scurvy, for James Lind's cure for ascorbic-acid deficiency was not yet to hand. The British Admiralty did not require a compulsory ration of lemons or limes until 1795.

The second wartime hazard was most peculiar, and most peculiar to these colonies. If you remained a civilian, you could add a powerful incentive to a death wish by becoming a Loyalist. General Washington's merciless edict against Loyalist soldiers— "no terms, no amnesty, no pardon"—was matched by the Congress with punitive laws against civilians that seized your property, deprived you of the vote and the protection of the courts, disqualified you from any profession, and put you into a detention camp. You were also, as long as you were at large, at the mercy of manic patriots, guerrilla bands that roamed the cities and, if they caught you, stripped you and either tarred and feathered you or ran you on rails out of town. In about half the states, these vigilantes assumed the authority to hang you. The enormous number of over 200,000 Loyalists, about one-fifteenth of the whole colonial population, died or were beaten up or forcibly exiled, or voluntarily fled the country.

It is an early and ugly passage in the history of the United States and one regularly glossed over in the books. I doubt it is being taught in our schools just now as a cautionary patriotic tale.

I appreciate that all these generalizations I have called on make more of a catalogue than a picture—a practice that accords with the method of the most respectable historians. I have followed it, I'm afraid, because I am in the presence of an audience of professionals. But now I must, as an amateur, take a flier at a very unacademic experiment; which is to imagine the life of one Philadelphia family living through the Revolutionary War. My inclination to do this is determined, I'm sure, by a temperamental prejudice, acquired long ago as a history student, in favor of people like Cicero and G. M. Trevelyan and Samuel Eliot Morison as against—or should I say, alongside—Benedetto Croce and Theodor Mommsen. (Mommsen, after all, called Cicero "a journalist in the worst sense of the word," a title which I for one should be proud to share with that noble Roman.) There are, it seems to me, several occupational conventions of the professional historian that an amateur, writing for a general audience, has a duty to flout. The first, which I dare to say is especially in evidence in this country, is to make a point, for the sake of a scholarly reputation, of not writing in plain English. Then to demonstrate one's expertise by manipulating the professional jargon. Then to marshal as many facts as possible and attest them in reams of footnotes, the whole presenting in the end not a plausible fantasy of life in another age but something closer to what the bankers call a trial balance. Too often the effect on the reader is that of scanning a huge and accurate index of a book whose main text has been mislaid.

What I want to do, on the contrary, is to try and give you the *feel* of the facts, a sense of living in that time and experiencing in the flesh and the spirit the normal hazards to survival. So, since I have no academic reputation to protect, no "tenure" to imperil, I mean to put you in Philadelphia in 1776 as a fairly representative man. I say "man," rather than "person," because I'm thinking of a father, then and until recently known as the head of the family: a family man of what we should call the upper middle class. At the start, then, you are privileged to escape the chronic afflictions of poverty.

Imagine that you are a Philadelphia patriot in 1776. You are in the dye trade, an exporter of indigo. You would be in trouble right away, because of the withdrawal of the British bounty and the difficulty of getting the stuff up from South Carolina and especially from Georgia, which was in the midst of a civil war. These misfortunes would amount to as much anxiety as you could handle in your office by day. On your way home in the evening, your revolutionary loyalty would be slightly confused by having to pass by two recruiting stations: one for the Continental Army, the other for the "True Philadelphians" signing up for the King's service. You have two sons. (You have had five children in all. A son died in infancy, a daughter two years later of diphtheria. You have, as a pride and joy, a pretty and a healthy daughter who is busy just now at a patriots' canteen brewing cups of tea—Dutch tea I hasten to say—and listening to the troubles of the men who long to be home in Maryland or in the Western—that is to say, the Appalachian—mountains.)

Both sons are of military age. The younger is aflame with gaudy dreams of an America in which the pursuit of happiness will be unencumbered by a British garrison, by blue laws, or by taxes in any form. He is a first-rate romantic and a brave boy, and he has amazed his chums by signing up for a whole year, pay or no pay. He takes a disgusted view of the Connecticut militia, which threatened to march home in a body when no bounty was forthcoming and had to be quelled, or quieted, by the personal entreaty of General Washington. Washington is your boy's idol, and in conversation with recalcitrant recruits he would quote with scornful relish Washington's despairing line about the lax limits of military service: "We have found it as practicable to stop a torrent as these people when their time is done."

Your elder son is a little more complexly embittered. He had gone off for a time, well before the war, as a surveyor's apprentice in western Virginia; he had had one sickening brush with the Indians, enough anyway to stamp traumatically on his memory the sight of a headless baby, and of a farming family sitting in a stupor beside the ashes of the farmhouse and the bones of burned animals. He is inclined to share the Quaker feeling about fighting of any kind. But the rumors, whether true or not—and most of them are well substantiated—of the British systematically arming the Indians are enough for him. So he had enlisted too, but only for a month at a time. However, when he found that he would have to buy his own uniform, and then the first month's pay was three months overdue, he quit. So now he is something of a grumbler around the house.

Your best friend is an importer in the English trade, shipping furniture and cutlery out of Bristol and the port of London. He was at first very anxious to retain his business and therefore was a determined Tory, until he met in Philadelphia a Spanish businessman who assured him that once the British were beaten, he would have a new market in the eastern branch of New Spain, reaching from the Appalachians a thousand miles into the interior. So, taking this tide in anticipation of its flood, he began importing olives from Spain and very sensibly turned patriot. And nobody is now a more fervent reciter of the more inflamed passages of Tom Paine and Thomas Jefferson during twilight sojourns at the Indian Queen Tavern.

But you have another friend to whom you have long been devoted for his fair-mindedness and an indefinable charm of character. He is a lawyer, and he has incurred the suspicion of the local patriots for having engaged in a long correspondence with an English friend in one of the Inns of Court. He had assured the English when the troubles began that the coming Declaration of Independence would be full of fustian and preposterous rhetoric about the alleged tyrannies of old Farmer

George, the homely and bewildered monarch who was more than ever at the mercy of witless ministers only theoretically of his own choice. Your friend knew in his bones that reason and equity would prevail, and there would be no war. And even though he deplored the closing of the port of Boston by London as an act of massive stupidity, he has remained a Loyalist still. He is a man of immovable convictions, and his convictions are to be his ruin. Soon there will be talk of sequestration laws, and your friend will be sent off to a detention camp, while his house, his practice, and his goods will be seized. In the end, he will be allowed to get out to the West Indies, to start all over again, and his wife will die there of yellow fever. All this is in the future, but you are fearful for him. When it is all over, the bleakest memory of the war will come to be that of the day when you saw him and his family, with a sackful of possessions, going off to a detention camp in the mountains.

But for now, there are more pressing sorrows. A smallpox epidemic comes roaring up the coast and takes a heavy toll, in Baltimore, Philadelphia, and New York. The families in your neighborhood are put into quarantine, which means that your business is at a standstill and you have to ration your store of food. For you and yours, the quarantine—which was never too effective anyway—comes too late. Your pretty daughter is scarred for life, and you begin to revise your dreams of her as a bouncing wife and mother. Into the quarantine compound, as always into any isolated community, drift lurid speculations about which side who is on, about friends dead or defected, about neighbors railroaded out of town on the word of some influential gossip. Once the quarantine is lifted, your patriotism is further tested by tavern talk of a secret committee which meets in Philadelphia with French booksellers and Spanish businessmen, an intrigue that is rendered more frightening by the suspicion that some of these foreign agents are plants, or double agents, of the British. Then, one day, you receive a confidential message and a mysteriously sealed order, which enables you to deliver a cargo of indigo to the sloop *Reprisal,* berthed in the port of Philadelphia. You discover later that this was made possible by the fact of Benjamin Franklin's being aboard, off on one of his secret missions to enlist the backing of the French. And you hear later from Franklin's own lips the interesting, if irrelevant, intelligence that throughout the voyage he was in a bad way with gout and what he called "the boils." Also, the chickens and turkeys aboard were too much for his bleeding teeth, so he had survived for thirty-nine days on salt beef. As the months go by, news—always dramatic and always good—comes in about American victories in battles that seem as far away as Europe: in Vermont, Massachusetts, and Long Island.

The war had always seemed to be far off until, in the dark winter of 1777-78, the British bore down on the city and there was nothing else to do but follow the Congress in its retreat to the hills. And here you would run into yet another of those maddening vicissitudes of war that do not make smooth lyrics for patriotic tunes. You had naturally assumed that one asset of being forced into the country would be an easier access to the farmers' food. In fact, you find fresh food harder to come by, since so many farmers were daytime patriots who shipped their produce by night to the British army of occupation in Philadelphia, which paid handsomely for it. In that ghastly winter, you see more friends go down with typhus. Dysentery is a part of daily life. Even Washington's army, in its muddy or frozen encampment, has no practical medical services, and you learn to lock and bar your cottage doors against the depredations of deserters.

But you count yourself lucky in having in your camp one doctor who has had the sense to forget, for the duration of the emergency anyway, his former preoccupation with exhalations and fluxes and has reverted to Wesley's simple practices and the collection of herbs. You have time now to sit and brood over your own quick passage from the first glow of independence to the anxieties of epidemics and bad business, and that troublesome elder son. He grew to be so enraged by the desertions and chronic corruption of the army that he took off for Vermont, only to learn that his new hero, the gallant Ethan Allen, was a prisoner of the British in Montreal. He stayed there until Allen's release and then was exasperated to find himself a member of an army secretly arranging to turn Vermont into a British state when the war was over. He became disillusioned yet again when the Vermont Fuehrer fled from his beloved state to avoid imprisonment for debt. When at last the war did end, your son would stand trial, but a little desperate pull would get him acquitted of the charge of treason. And you reflect, a little ruefully, that your elder son, like many another born loser disguised as an idealist, has a knack for picking people and situations that will let him down.

This is not an unduly glum or melodramatic picture of one family's life and the way it would go from the exhilaration of independence to the reality of the morning after. Well, at the end of it all, you and your wife would be, by God's grace with the assistance of Dr. Wesley, fairly healthy and stoical. Your daughter will marry happily. The younger son has a permanent limp from a wound at Brandywine, and the elder son appears still to be ready for new crusades, or disappointments, with other heroes. Your wife will astound everybody by living into her late seventies, a very great age in those days. You yourself will be carried off in your sixties by the yellow fever epidemic of 1793. You will be unceremoniously buried at night by two men, one chewing madly on garlic, the other digging with one hand holding to his nose a handkerchief soaked in vinegar.

I hope this picture has modified, on this happy occasion, any tendency to simplify the Revolution into a holy crusade, and the life lived under it into a round of martial triumphs accompanied by an offstage civilian chorus bellowing "The Joys of

Liberty." I hope it is not too hackneyed to say, at the end, that life in 1776 was as cheerful and grim and exhilarating and testy, and comic and tragic, as it is today. What Lester King says about doctors could be said too of lawyers, landowners, farmers, businessmen, all the rest of us: "In the eighteenth century, doctors were just as clever as they are today, just as perceptive and clear-thinking, exerting powers of observation and inference just as keen. At the same time, eighteenth-century physicians were quite as muddle-headed, obtuse, grasping, prejudiced, and contentious as their descendants."

As for health and endurance—whether you were buoyed up by the consolations of a religious faith or were just a normal secular heathen—the likeliest guarantee rested as always with the luck of choosing the right parents. And even if you had started with the right genes, the only reliable recipe for a long and comfortable life, then as now, was to be healthy, wealthy, and unprincipled.

How It All Ended

GIVEN AT THE STATE DEPARTMENT, WASHINGTON, D.C.,
AT A DINNER CELEBRATING THE TWO HUNDREDTH
ANNIVERSARY OF THE SIGNING OF THE TREATY OF PARIS,
OCTOBER 6, 1983

How It All Ended

Of course, I'm proud that you should call on a mere reporter to celebrate so majestic an event in American history, and I take it that this invitation is a graceful way of paying tribute to the profession of journalism itself.

In the recent past, American journalists have done yeoman service—whatever that means—in shaping American history, or at least bending it their way. I recall the man who needled President Nixon at a press conference, with ultimately dire consequences for the party of the first part. And another fine reporter (whom I'm tickled to see here tonight) once held a courteous inquisition, masquerading as an interview, with a prominent United States Senator and thereby effectively removed him from the presidential race. But journalists have not only made history, they have been distinguished, though not always conspicuous, for solving some baffling historical puzzles. Fifty years ago this month, the late Robert Benchley cleared up a mystery that had racked the Western world when he published his famous confession, which began: "Let's have an end of all this shilly-shallying. *I* killed Rasputin."

More recently, dogged and courageous research has been done by Calvin Trillin on what turns out to be the myth that the Pilgrim Fathers sat down at the end of the harvest and instituted the tradition of serving turkey as the prime Thanksgiving dish. As Trillin has lately proved beyond all dispute, it was the Indians who, as invited guests to that feast, brought along the quintessential American dish, which they had learned from their ancestors, who had picked it up in turn from none other than Christopher Columbus. (The Indians, we are told, did not call him Christopher Columbus; they called him "the big Italian fella.") Anyway, as Trillin rightly says, Columbus "did not come all the way to this country just to have a town in Ohio named after him. And rather than eat any morsel of English Puritan cuisine . . . he would sooner have agreed that the world was shaped like an isosceles triangle." So it was his descendants who introduced the first, the true, Thanksgiving dish: spaghetti carbonara (with specially imported prosciutto), which the English hated, calling it "heretically tasty." It appears that the misapprehension—which has caused and propagated the myth down all these centuries—set in shortly after the Indians bade their hosts goodbye. On the way back to their pads, their chief said: "What a bunch of turkeys!"

I'm afraid I can't offer anything as incisive or brilliant in my own revisionist version of the Treaty of Paris, but I shall do my damnedest. There are, I believe, at least seven so-called Treaties of Paris. Identifying which one you are talking about can be almost as tricky as getting the proper directions to "Inspiration Point." You may think you are being guided to the peak of the High Sierras, only to find yourself climbing a hill on Staten Island. We are talking, then, about the treaty concluded between Britain, the United States, France, and Spain which put the seal on the final terms agreed to on the previous 20th of January, the date that marked the end of hostilities everywhere. (For fifteen months after the surrender at Yorktown, the French, the Spanish, and the Dutch were still banging away at the Brits, in naval battles mostly, all the way between the West Indies and the Balearics. But American children are taught that the fighting ended with Cornwallis's surrender; which only shows a lively appreciation that you can forget about the smaller fry once you've bumped off the big English fella in North America.) *The* treaty, then, was signed in Paris on the 3rd of September, 1783.

The date may bring up—among mathematicians present—the question: what are we doing here a month too late? Well, it seems to me right on, in accordance with a venerable British tradition that has caused, and still causes, indecent amusement among visiting colonials to Britain. Look at it this way. The college end-of-year dances at Cambridge (England) are called May Week Balls *because* they take place in June. By an extension of the same tradition, the Earl of Leicester lives not in Leicestershire but in Norfolk. And the Duke of Norfolk, naturally, in Sussex. And if the Queen of England, who was born on the 21st of April, can celebrate her birthday annually in June, it is in the blood tradition that we should celebrate the signing of the Declaration of Independence on the 4th of July, since it was signed on the 2nd. And that, tonight, we should be hailing the Treaty of Paris on the 6th of October, because it was concluded and signed on the 3rd of September.

Well, on an occasion like this, a joyful dinner party, you don't want to be subjected to an Op-Ed-page sermon or bothered with niggling documentary details of my herculean research into how the Revolutionary War was won, and who got what from the treaty. You want, I believe, the gist. Well, here it is. Or, rather, there are two gists. And the first one will explain why it was the French, quite rightly, who had most to say about the negotiating and distribution of the loot.

We have to go back to Paris in the middle of the war and the two characters who, probably more than any soldier, were to decide its outcome. One was King Louis the Sixteenth, a French investment banker and—sure—a tyrant, who was married to Marie (Let Them Eat Certificates of Deposit) Antoinette.

Louis was, however, young and weak, whereas the American representative in Paris was old and wise. He was one Benjamin Franklin, the inventor of the lightning rod and also the King's adviser on mesmerism. Anyway, Franklin was able to mesmerize the King with the dazzling prospect of rebuilding the forts along the Appalachians and collaring the river trade down the Mississippi—if only the King would bail out the bankrupt American revolutionaries and then bring his armies in on their side. Franklin, I'm sorry to say, had no latter-day illusions about allying yourself only with nations that are charter members of the American Civil Liberties Union. He cajoled and wheedled, and behaved like anything but a boy from Philadelphia who had so long before put out a calendar of moral maxims, like "Early to bed, early to rise" and "He that goes a-borrowing goes a-sorrowing." He felt no pain in proposing to borrow on a whopping scale. The King was charmed by him and came through with gifts and loans worth fifty-five million livres, and then with his armies. So, just when General Washington found himself stuck in a Pennsylvania quagmire, his army disastrously thinned from desertions and exhausted from hunger and dysentery, the French came in. And from then on, it was all up with the British.

The fact that the French—not to put too fine a point on it—won the Revolutionary War is not, you'll have noticed, the main theme of American school textbooks. I am sorry that the French ambassador could not be here tonight, but it is a pleasure to see his deputy chief of staff. If it hadn't been for the French, *we* wouldn't be here tonight. Or, we'd more likely be repledging our allegiance to Elizabeth the Second in the presence of our Lord and Master—Mistress—Maggie Thatcher.

The second gist has to do with the treaty negotiations and another boon the French conferred on the Americans—and, incidentally, on the British. It could explain the absence tonight of the Spanish ambassador. In the nearly two years of haggling over who should do what to whom, it was the French who told the Spanish to stop going on about Gibraltar—which they'd been besieging—and take Florida instead. The Spanish were always great realtors (the word comes from them—I guess—El Realtor!). They jumped at it. They took Florida, not knowing that Andrew Jackson was in the offing. He was a soldier with, you might say, no very respectful sense of history. At any rate, he was not of Mr. Begin's cast of mind. He saw no reason why Indian tribes that had been born here and lived here for fifteen thousand years had prior rights of ownership. And even when the Supreme Court ruled that the Seminoles and the Creeks and the Cherokees owned their lands in Florida and Georgia and must stay on them, Jackson did something that many a later president must have longed to do. He said, "Shucks!"—to the Supreme Court. "Get them Indians out." Which the army did. As for the Spanish, Jackson looked around and was amazed to see them still there. He said (I quote from his secret diary): "Who *are* these people? Spanish? What are they doing here? Don't they know this is America?" So he kicked *them* out. Two hundred years later, they discovered they not only didn't have Florida. They don't have Gibraltar.

Talking of absent friends, we ought to recall that when Benjamin West arranged a sitting to paint a group portrait of the signatories to the treaty, the only delegate missing was the British delegate. He wasn't late. He hadn't forgotten the date. He had discovered that being beaten was a contingency not mentioned in the King's regulations. Talk about a treaty of friendship! He was one sore diplomat, I can tell you. He is represented in West's sketch painting (as you can see in the adjoining room) by a veil or smear of ectoplasm. And I think we ought to pay special tribute to the present British ambassador. I think it was, to coin a phrase, jolly sporting of him to consent to be with us tonight.

Well, that's the true story.

A month or so ago, the Keeper of the Public Record Office

in London arrived in New York with the original treaty and, on behalf of the British government, presented it for display in the Museum of the City of New York, to a noted American Anglophile, Ed Koch. At the ceremony, Mayor Koch behaved impeccably, as always, but was seen to be reading with his lips the opening sentence, apparently memorizing its style for future employment in signing a contract with, say, the Teamsters. It begins:

> It having pleased the Divine Providence to dispose the Heart of the most Serene and most Potent Prince George the Third [he was nuts at the time] by the Grace of God, King of Great Britain, France and Ireland, Defender of the Faith, Duke of Brunswick and Luxembourg, Arch-Treasurer and Prince Elector of the Holy Roman Empire [on the one hand] and of the United States of America [on the other] to forget all past misunderstandings and differences that have unhappily interrupted the good Correspondence and Friendship which they mutually wish to restore; and to establish such a beneficial and satisfactory Intercourse between the two Countries upon the ground of reciprocal advantages and mutual convenience as may promote and secure to both perpetual Peace and Harmony. . . .

So be it. Now let us say good night but not goodbye. I hope we shall meet again six years from now, in 1989, to celebrate the real American Bicentennial: the final adoption of the American Constitution and of the system of government that has staggered through, bloody but unbowed, to this day.

In the meantime, some of you may be wondering what a young man thinking of majoring in history, and changing his mind, recently wondered to me. Why, since July 1976, have we spent so much time with fiddling celebrations of the triumphant anniversaries of American history while all of us, in every land, burn with fear of annihilation and the end of human history altogether? I offered him what I offer you: a memory from the Revolutionary War I dug up almost forty years ago from the records of the Connecticut House of Representatives. Incidentally, may I now humbly sneak in on the company of Messrs. Rather, Mudd, Benchley, and Trillin and disclose for the first time how one journalist managed to elect a President of the United States, if by a fly's-wing majority? I printed this memoir in a book published in 1952. Eight years later, it was brought to the attention of the Democratic nominee for the presidency, and he read it to wet-eyed audiences up and down the campaign trail. Finally, to tumultuous applause, he read it word for word (without credit) as the peroration of his last, televised, campaign speech in Madison Square Garden. It was not, however, included in the release of his text. Here it is.

> The time was the 19th of May, 1780. The place was Hartford, Connecticut. The day has gone down in New England history as a terrible foretaste of Judgment Day. For at noon the skies turned from blue to gray and by midafternoon had blackened over so densely that, in that religious age, men fell on their knees and begged a final blessing before the end came. The Connecticut House of Representatives was in session. And as some men fell down and others clamored for an immediate adjournment, the Speaker of the House, one Colonel Davenport, came to his feet. He silenced them and said these words: "The Day of Judgment is either approaching or it is not. If it is not, there is no cause for adjournment. If it is, I choose to be found doing my duty. I wish, therefore, that candles may be brought."

We can't do much better than that. Ladies and gentlemen, let candles be brought.

A Crash Course in Americanism

GIVEN AT WOLSEY HALL, NEW HAVEN, IN RESPONSE TO
THE PRESENTATION, BY PRESIDENT KINGMAN BREWSTER,
OF YALE UNIVERSITY'S HOWLAND MEDAL, APRIL 19, 1977

A Crash Course in
Americanism

Many years ago, when I was still fairly new to this country, I asked my guru, Mr. H. L. Mencken, why American universities were overrun every spring by hundreds of recipients of honorary degrees who were not noticeably scholars or distinguished authors or scientists. "It's a form," he said, "of certifying a pompous ass. If I had my way, no man would ever be given a degree he hadn't worked to earn. Honorary degrees are fit only for realtors, chiropractors, and Presidents of the United States."

This dreadful stigma stuck in the back of my mind for years and was uncomfortably retrieved when I in my turn—and especially in the Bicentennial year—found myself gasping in a flood of invitations to receive honorary degrees from universities and colleges as far apart as Alaska and that junior college in Texas where Lyndon Johnson once taught (I kid you not) elocution. I had talked there during the Second War and had not been going for more than three minutes before a strapping young Texan got up and asked in the kindliest way: "Sir, would you mahnd mod'ratin' yore acc-sent?"

My reluctance to accept an honorary degree was reinforced only a few years ago by the late Stephen Potter when an invitation came to me from St. Andrews, which is the oldest university in

Scotland and—even more to the point—is only about a three-iron shot from the Old Course. As a golfing nut, Potter was acutely sympathetic to my problem. He said, "Frightful dilemma! The trouble is that taking an honorary degree is rather like being knighted. It stamps you forever as an okay chap." I yielded nonetheless, and pretty soon found myself threatened by that ceremony which requires the Queen of England to strike you on the shoulder with a sword, but—as Noel Coward said— "very gently, thank God."

I have put up a dogged resistance ever since, except to the university of my native city, Manchester, which I feared would take a dim view of a local boy who had demonstrably got too big for his britches. But however much I may have rationalized my distaste for becoming either a certified pompous ass or an okay chap, I have to admit that in private moments what really rankled was the fact that I had never received the call from my two old schools: from Cambridge or from Yale. Now, it has happened.

I claim Yale as my American *alma mater* whether or not Yale claims me. So much so that when at the end of the first year of my Commonwealth Fellowship I had to transfer to Harvard, I said to one of my friends—who may well be here—"By now, I'm thoroughly at home here. New Haven will always be the American cradle. I have made fine friends here, and now I have to start all over again in a college in some God-forsaken place in the frozen north that was started with one house, one-eighth of an acre, and two cows." He said, rather cryptically, "If you feel that way now, you'll certainly be a better Yale man after spending a year at Harvard." This is a comforting psychological theory, but not without its perils. It reminds me of the young Jew who fell in love with a Catholic girl, whose parents forbade the match unless the boy took instruction. Which he did. But when the wedding day came he never showed up at the church. He sent a courier, however, with the message that

he had become so captivated by Catholicism that he'd decided
to become a priest.

It was suggested to me that I might like to talk about the
founding of Yale and its contributions to the Republic up to
and through the Bicentennial. Before you rush for the doors,
let me say that to expose you to an after-lunch speech on that
formidable topic would be carrying the First Amendment too
far. What did occur to me as more appropriate, and less long-
winded, would be to pay my respects to Yale with a piece of
psychohistory here revealed for the first time: my sudden and
involuntary crash course in Americanism. For it was here on a
single day in 1933 that an extremely nonpolitical Englishman
was given a shock treatment that spurred a lifelong interest in
American politics.

The day was Saturday, March the 4th, 1933, which the
historians among you will recall as the day of the first inaugu-
ration of Franklin Roosevelt, but which those of you who were
alive and sentient anywhere in the United States will remember
more indelibly as the Day the Money Stopped. There was no
negotiable currency. Everybody knew this except me, who had
never read any other page of *The New York Times* than the one
that carried the notices of Broadway plays. I did not possess a
radio even, for the only time I had switched on a neighbor's
set, I concluded that American radio existed as an audible branch
of advertising, given over at the time to extolling, through the
larynx of an impressive baritone, the virtues of a shaving cream.

On that morning, I took the train to New York to meet a
young Englishwoman coming in on a Cunarder, to put her up
for the weekend and—as we used to say—to "show her a good
time." May I dampen your ardor to be in on a bit of hanky-
panky by saying that I was at the time madly in love with another
young Englishwoman who was not, alas, coming in on a Cunarder or any other ship. Never was a more high-minded weekend spent by a male and a female in their early twenties. I had

in my pocket enough walking-around money to see me through the rest of the day. I met the boat, greeted the young lady, who was as excited at being initiated into the life of New York by a knowing guide as I was at showing her what was what. We shall go, I announced, to my usual hotel, cash a check, and set off around the town. At the Tudor Hotel, on Forty-second Street, I went directly to the cashier, who had known me by now for many months. Under his fascinated gaze, I wrote out with a flourish a check for the luxurious amount of, say, thirty dollars. "What," he said, "is this?" He couldn't possibly cash it. With well-modulated sarcasm (this was the heyday of Noel Coward) I said, "D'you imagine there's a bank anywhere in the United States that might have the kindness to cash this check?" No, he said. "Go and read the papers, sonny!" (This, remember, was forty-four years ago.)

Of course, he was right. I walked over to the newsstand and saw the blanketing headline: "Roosevelt to Be Inaugurated at Noon; Declares Moratorium on All Banks." Still, being full of the bounce and sassiness of youth, I was not going to be fazed by a cashier and a word whose meaning I was unacquainted with. I parked the girl in the lobby of the hotel, told her to eat, read, walk, do anything she wished till I could get to New Haven and back again. My ace up the sleeve was a commutation ticket, which the Commonwealth Fund had thoughtfully provided so that I could dash to New York as often as I pleased to see the new plays (I was attached, loosely, to the School of Drama). I got back to New Haven and went the rounds of my friends. Most of them were out, and two or three others could cough up no more than a dollar or two. Then I thought of another Fellow, a Yorkshireman. I was, remember, a native of Lancashire, which maintains an uneasy truce with its ancient enemy in the Wars of the Roses. I had been brought up to believe that all Yorkshiremen were lumbering, penny-pinching oafs who yet kept their money under the mattress. To my delight, my Yorkshireman in Harkness proved it. I accused him of his native stinginess and, with a blush, he lifted the mattress and exposed a nursery of the green stuff. From him, after heartbreaking pleas, I extracted three dollars. But I still had too little to get through the weekend. Whereupon I had the luck of a master stroke. I went in search of my first Yale friend, a man who had paid a courtesy call on me on my second night in New Haven. The last man I should ever have suspected of caginess or cunning, or of ever becoming a lawyer, or of developing the qualities required to recommend him to Lyndon Johnson as an Under Secretary of State. His name was— still is—Eugene V. Rostow.

He dashed my last hope by saying, "I haven't even got two dollars of my own." As I was about to say something final and asinine, like "Well, it doesn't matter, actually," he said, "Wait a minute. You are an editor of the *Hoot,* and I am *the* editor!" The *Harkness Hoot* was an undergraduate magazine as famous at the time, we all assumed, as the *American Mercury* or *Pravda.* Rostow then gave me a merry look and said the sentence that turned me from a theater director into a foreign correspondent. "Do you know," he said, "what a due bill is?" I didn't, but I soon learned. The St. Regis Hotel in New York, it came out, had an outstanding due bill with the *Hoot* for an advertisement inserted in the last issue at the agreed cost of one hundred dollars, which was at the time, I believe, the exact amount of the federal budget.

I took their bill, and took the train, whipped into the Tudor, and, with a passing sneer at the cashier, whisked my girl into a taxi and off to the St. Regis. It was difficult to get in against the outgoing tide of guests on their way home. We must have been the only new guests that day, and the reservations clerk was suspicious enough to call the manager. A dapper, gray-haired man appeared and looked in amused contempt at these two innocents. "Can I help you?" he asked, with the tone of a cop turning his flashlight on a burglar. I said we should like two nice rooms on a top floor. He reeled, but only for a moment. I presented my due bill, his due bill. He was immediately transformed, facing, perhaps, the only paid-up newcomers he had ever seen. He started clapping his hands like a flamenco dancer. Minions came running. We were put in a suite with two bedrooms. It cost, as I recall, something awful: eight, possibly ten dollars a night. And so we started to do the town.

I had bought, several weeks before, tickets to a first night: Jimmy Durante in a musical called *Strike Me Pink*. I had been struck pinker. But it was a tumultuous evening. The audience, including many strong men weeping onto their white ties and tails, would not settle to the opening chorus. So, evidently by some prearranged signal, the chorus girls broke their opening song, leaped to the front of the stage, and tapped out a routine and chanted in unison: "We depend on *Roose*velt, we depend on *him!*" The audience rose, barked and cheered, and collapsed comfortably into its seats. Durante rushed on, screamed, "Everywhere I go I find—chaos!" Robert Benchley wrote: "It practically marked the end of the Depression."

We danced all night. We dispensed carefree—twenty-five-cent—tips. I spent the next three months going through the checks in my depleted bank account and came on the reckoning, by way of taxi rides, a nightclub supper, a ride through Central Park, of the whole mad whirl: "To Helmut Schmidt, 45 cents"; "Antonio Colucci, 65 cents"; "Connie's Inn, $1.95." And so on. By twilight, at the latest, on that 4th of March, everybody was ready to take a check. I think it must have been about three months before I paid off my debt to the *Harkness Hoot,* for I had been seduced into my first all-American prejudice: the belief that once you have a credit card in your hand—or its old-fashioned equivalent—it is better than currency.

This memorable experience germinated a lively interest in the banking system, what was left of it. I started to read, at first casually and in later years voraciously, the various and ingenious ways in which different governors handled the moratorium. Governor Cross of Connecticut marched to his bank in full public view to make a deposit and thus arrest a popular run. On the other hand, Huey Long, the dictator of Louisiana, did it another way. He summoned the bank managers of Louisiana to a lavish dinner in the Roosevelt Hotel in New Orleans and the privilege of a night there as his guests. He wined and dined them abundantly and dismissed them, with hugs and cheerful reassurances, to their rooms. Where, no doubt simultaneously, they grabbed the telephones. But all the wires had been cut, and outside each bedroom the Kingfish had provided the courtesy of a bodyguard.

This unforgettable weekend taught me the priceless lesson, for a reporter, of what I might call the check and double check. Whenever a professor of political science explained to me exactly how some American institution worked, and certainly whenever a member of the administration—any administration—was expounding the wisdom of a current policy, I went off and checked with such as Mayor Kelly, or Jim Farley, or the opposition whips, or an aging newspaperman, or a Tammany chieftain, or the man who didn't get the nomination, or even a lowly precinct captain. Huey Long himself later explained, lying on a hotel bed and delicately picking his toenails, the way the poll tax could work in counties where it had been abolished. Many years later, after the presidential election of 1960, I was in Chicago and read, in some elaborate post-election tally, that one election district on the edge of beyond had given eighty votes for Kennedy and two for Nixon. I went off to look over this Kennedy stronghold and found a vacant lot with a gas station adjoining two crumbling houses, which could have contained, at most, a dozen qualified voters. That night, I asked a Cook County "judge" how come a district with no more than a dozen voters could give eighty votes to Kennedy and only two to Nixon. He heaved a great, tolerant sigh and said: "It's very simple. If there *had* been eighty-two voters, there would have been eighty for Kennedy and two for Nixon.''

And so, after six blind innocent months in America I discovered, on the 4th of March, 1933, the meaning of the word "moratorium"; I became a willing student of American politics, and an enthusiastic slave of an economic system whose main doctrine is "Live now, pay later if you feel like it."

It remains only for me to add a congratulatory word to your President on his appointment to the Court of St. James's, so called because the court moved from there in the eighteenth century. He will, I am sure, glorify a post too often dispensed by Presidents of the United States to heavy contributors to their maintenance. (The late Joseph Davies lusted after London, but Roosevelt—looking over the list of campaign contributors—decided he hadn't earned it; he would have to take Moscow.)

Speaking as an old ambassador-watcher, may I dare to wish Ambassador Brewster all the patience and stamina he will need to withstand the round of parties given to celebrate the separate national holidays of the—is it?—one hundred and ninety-odd countries represented in the London diplomatic establishment. If he begins to grow weary at the end of any week during which he has had to lunch the most prosperous leather manufacturer in Pennsylvania, the chairwoman of the Mobile Camelia Society, the secretary of the Daughters of the American Revolution, the Democratic chairman of Brewster County, Texas, the holder of the Jaguar franchise for southern Georgia—I hope he will seek consolation from the warning of a former distinguished ambassador to London: "The two things you must acquire in this job are a perpetual grin and a lead stomach."

Finally, I hope I have said enough to show that as a knockabout historian—an amateur talking to a professional elite—I have at least a debatable claim on this splendid medal.

Thoughts Coming Out of the Ether

GIVEN BEFORE THE ROYAL COLLEGE OF SURGEONS,
LONDON, NOVEMBER 12, 1975

Thoughts Coming Out of
the Ether

I am aware that I am facing an assembly of experts—licensed experts, anyway—who, like all specialists, will permit ad-libbing only inside their own trade union. I think you might give me a sympathetic hearing if I were to think aloud about inflation, municipal bankruptcy, politicians, détente, and other humdrum evils. You might even listen respectfully if I reverted to my old trade as a foreign correspondent and reported as faithfully as I could on the two balky questions that are fretting your brethren in the United States, which, put in the simplest philosophical terms, are: what is the act of malpractice? and when does death take place? or, in the case of barely sentient human vegetables—not to mention such a determined immortal as Generalissimo Franco—when should mortality be allowed to settle in? The latter puzzle is one that has graveled doctors at least since the time of Seneca. Lately, it has been complicated everywhere by the growth of medical technology and in the United States by the teasing variety of state laws, whereby, for instance, in New York life is—at the moment—the existence of a heartbeat and in some other states a brainwave.

But I am pretty sure that you are not going to take from *me* airy spontaneities about the thyroglossal duct, the Pfannenstiel incision, or why nurses in attendance in the early days of thoracic surgery got a curious infection of the fingertips. So I am literally going to watch my words!

Mr. President, when you invited me to give this address I accepted with alacrity and without a second thought. It was only a week or two ago that I began to examine the motives behind such an eager acceptance. I don't know that this is ever a wise thing to do after the age of fifty, or after you have got off the analytic couch once and for all. You have to show *something* for all those years lived or for all that money down the drain. We must all pretend that there comes a time when we are well aware of our limitations and can live with them, that we are ready not to fight our neurosis but to ride in tandem with it.

Well, I decided that my motive in saying yes to you was very similar to that of anxious intellectuals who steep themselves in the Freudian literature in the unconscious hope of insulating themselves from the need for treatment. In other words, my appearance here is an interesting (I hope) example of the theme on which I had the honor, two years ago, to address your physician colleagues: a disguised symptom of hypochondriasis—exactly the same process as that whereby a person wincing with alarming symptoms goes to the doctor, has a thorough examination, and loses the symptoms. I feel that so long as I am in your presence a knife will be called upon to do service only in conjunction with a fork.

When I first met Mr. Robert McNamara, the present head of the World Bank, he was the United States Secretary of Defense and already deeply embroiled in the Vietnam adventure. He had just then come back from one of those missions to the battlefield which, at regular intervals for the next six or seven years, bucked up the White House with the assurance that the tunnel had definitely appeared at the end of the light—or the other way round, I forget now. I asked him how, in the first place, he had gone about getting an elementary grasp of the history and plight of Vietnam once the dreadful problem had been handed to him. "It was simple," he said, "I took out the twenty-third volume of the *Encyclopaedia Britannica* and looked up Vietnam."

If this is the way a statesman begins to learn about a war before, in fact, taking it over, it certainly did not seem too naive a precedent for a layman about to address an audience of surgeons. So *I* took out the twenty-first volume of the *Encyclopaedia Britannica*, which begins with Sordello (the thirteenth-century Italian troubadour) and ends with Textile Printing (which, as you probably already knew, is "the application of art and science in the production of designs on any fibrous materials without resource [*sic*] to embroidering or appliquéing").

Our own subject appears near the middle of the gamut. "SURGERY," it says, "The treatment of malformations and diseases by manual operation." A rather puzzling definition to me. Because once, in Palm Springs, California, when I had a good old muscle spasm in the lower back, I went for the first—and I may say the last—time to a chiropractor. His "manual operations" so aggravated the existing malfunction that I staggered off to a surgeon in San Francisco who—since he was a good friend of mine—felt no compulsion to assert his status by seizing a knife. But he did tell me that a good deal of his practice—practice, that is, in what *he* called surgery—was devoted to repairing the damage done by these same muscle men and piano heavers whom the *Britannica* defines as surgeons.

Obviously, I am getting no help from boning up. So it seems better to throw myself on your attention for a little while and try to do what I once did to the staff of the Mayo Clinic: to let you in on the secret (to which experts in any closed profession can be oblivious for a lifetime)—the secret of what the layman thinks of *you*.

I doubt there is a profession other than yours—unless it is that of a burglar with a revolver—that is less likely to see its clients as reasonable human beings alive and kicking and possessed of free will. People may confidently boo a comedian, argue with a lawyer, haggle with a shopkeeper, and reveal to a spouse, a lover, or a friend the whole range of their character from the adorable to the detestable. But when a man goes to the doctor his character is inhibited by anxiety. When he appears before a consulting surgeon what you see is a homunculus cowed by fright. Only a few weeks ago a journalist friend of mine suffering from disturbing symptoms was put into the hospital to be photographed and filtered and purged and tapped and distilled. And at the end of it his doctor for the past twenty-five years said, "What's the matter with you? Where is the insouciance that I so enjoy in those pieces you write for *The New Yorker*?" My friend said, "Insouciance be damned! What you are seeing is a bothered man."

Before we come to the special reputation of the surgeon among the laity it's only fair to say that doctors in general provoke in the rest of mankind a very ambivalent attitude of alternating awe and distrust. The moment a man hangs out his shingle and can call himself "Doctor," he is endowed by simple-minded people—grocers, elevator men, bus drivers, old ladies—with an occult insight into many things outside medicine: "Good morning, doctor, you think it'll rain today? . . ." "Your car is ready, doctor. . . ." "Doctor, is the government going to fall?"

I am aware that in this country *your* peculiar title [i.e., Mr.] is apt to blind ordinary people to your omniscience, but I am sure you contrive to let it leak out that you are technically entitled to the same wide-eyed respect as physicians. This deference is, however, a precautionary cover-up: one day the bowing doorman may need you. And when he does he will need you in a hurry.

But away from your presence, wherever two or three ordinary mortals are gathered together and the general topic of medicine and medical men comes up, I regret to tell you that chuckling skepticism is the most familiar mood by which the layman—the healthy layman—compensates for the infuriating fact that to him your expertise is a closed book. Nothing is more popular among educated people than the revelation that some greatly advertised medical breakthrough is a breakdown, even though these same people are at all times touchingly susceptible to reports of a new dramatic surgical technique, a foolproof diet, a miracle vitamin. They defend their own readiness to believe a quack by saying, "Look how they ridiculed Jenner, Pasteur, Lister, and Ehrlich." The trick, which is always impossible to perform at the time, is to demonstrate that the quacks are not Jenner, Pasteur, Lister, or Ehrlich.

For several years, in my late twenties and early thirties, friends of mine liked to coax me into telling the story of my first encounter with a radiologist. I had picked up some germ that was roaming around London, and when the X-rays came back the radiologist had appended a note which said: "The costal calcification of this patient is that of man of about fifty-five. However, the admission card gives the patient's age as twenty-seven. We attach no pathological significance to this discrepancy." I memorized that, and I can only say that if I now possess the costal calcification of a man of ninety-five I hope they still find nothing pathological about it.

And—as another example of the layman's delight in the discomfiture of doctors—I don't think, in my reporting days, I ever covered a story that produced such a Hallelujah Chorus of approving fan mail as the one about Javier Pereira, a peasant from Colombia, who was brought to New York by some promoter of a comic strip or chili-bean diet to attest the man's claim that he had been born in the year George Washington died and was therefore then 158 years old.

They put him into New York Hospital and called in the experts from Cornell Medical School. When they were done with him he was released to the press. He was just over four feet high, had hunched shoulders, the complexion of an alligator, and otherwise looked as hardy as a sick chicken. He was also no respecter of the press and took several quick lunges and sideswipes at anybody who came near, including a confident girl reporter who offered him a tender embrace and was felled by an uppercut to the nose. We all eventually calmed down for the reading of the report of the body of experts. It said—what we'd already deduced—that he was "vigorous, alert, and observing. His hands suffer from degenerative arthritis, but his bones are in a condition any young man might envy. Nonmedical evidence"—we loved that—"nonmedical evidence indicates that Mr. Pereira is indeed a very old man and quite possibly he may be more than 150 years of age. . . . Medical science at present possesses no methods of determining the exact age of any adult." The conclusion of this historic medical document was that he was four feet four inches tall and weighed eighty pounds. He was also alive.

I gather from your own response to this episode that in medicine—just as in the professions of industry, politics, music, the theater, university scholarship—there is plenty of intramural fun and games available at the expense of somebody else's specialty.

But if physicians are figures of fun to the layman (except when he needs them), what are we to say about the general view of surgeons? It is a long view and a bilious one.

The ancient Chinese made a proverb of the observation that you couldn't be a good surgeon until you yourself had been knifed. Two thousand or more years ago the layman's prejudice was brutally summarized by the old Greek who reported that when Acestorides died after an operation the surgeon excused himself by saying, "If he had lived the poor fellow would have been lame." And although, out of the literature of seven hundred years, you could compile an anthology of medical compliments to the delicate fingers and steady hands of surgeons, this standard flattery is punctured at regular intervals by the sniping malice of the layman: "A blind man works on wood as a surgeon on the body when he is ignorant of anatomy." And the first omen of an approaching malpractice suit comes in the bitter comment of John Earle, writing just after Shakespeare's time: "His [the surgeon's] gaines are very ill got, for he lives by the hurts of the Common-wealth ... and he holds a patient longer than our Courts a Cause." No question about it, if the family doctor is still looked on in many places as Dr. Jekyll, the surgeon is always secretly feared—in Britain especially—as *Mr.* Hyde.

A great deal of this popular suspicion is, I am sure, a spill-over from your traditional low reputation down the centuries in the medical profession itself. Dr. Guido Majno has recently told us, in his beautiful inquiry into healing in the ancient world,* that the Egyptians in their prime had over 130 surgical instruments. But so late as a century ago the ordinary GP could think of an amputation as a death warrant and point to the 50 percent mortality rate among compound fractures. Only a hundred years ago exactly Sir John Erickson announced to a respectful audience of his peers that operative surgery had achieved "its finality" and that surgical skill must forever stop short at the brain, the chest, and the abdomen. Today, on the contrary, the layman tends to assume that surgery needn't stop short at anything.

But I have to confess that the force of the folk maxim "Use the knife and lose a life" was so strong in me only twenty years ago that when I went to a distinguished New York surgeon— whose specialty was dignified among the Egyptians by the title Shepherd of the Anus—and when he looked me over and said, "We're going to wait and see, because scar tissue isn't as good as what God gave you and I think you ought to understand that *surgery is defeat,*" he was my man from then on.

Well, it occurs to me, perhaps a little belatedly, that you didn't come here to be insulted. But stay, ladies and gentlemen,

---

The Healing Hand: Man and Wound in the Ancient World (Cambridge, Mass.: Harvard University Press, 1975).

there is—and this time I'm sure of the sequence of the meta-
phor—there is light at the end of the tunnel. In the past ten or
twenty years there has occurred a most dramatic change in the
climate of popular opinion about surgeons; perhaps because
surgery itself has achieved such dramatically radical triumphs.
The layman may barely sense that he is living in the golden age
of cardiology, but television drama and even the television news
programs convince him that there is a DeBakey or a Barnard
in every hospital. Indeed, we have come to expect so much from
you that I myself hope to be alive to hear of the implanting of
the brain of a statesman in the cranium of a politician. I have
noticed that many ordinary educated people who a generation
ago assumed that antibiotics cured everything now talk about
hearts and kidneys as so many second-hand automobiles, to be
traded in for new ones at the end of the year.

Everyone yearns for an instant cure, and surgery appears
lately to offer it in a glamorous and spectacular way. And luckily
this new reputation is likely to be sustained not only by what
the layman knows but also by what he doesn't know. He doesn't
know, for example, that there are fashions in surgery. He would
have to fish out from a medical journal the dismaying news that
when, one year, there was a vogue for doing carotid endarter-
ectomies on people who had had strokes one hospital in California did 115 of them; but the next year, by which time the
literature had "cooled," it did only three. By now only a few
oldsters like me can claim to have been the victims of the American appendectomy mania. It was in New Haven, Connecticut,
forty-two years ago. I mention the date because it was a time
in America when you were whipped into surgery the moment
the first wave of peristalsis began to wash past McBurney's point.
Major Eisenhower, having nothing to do one rainy afternoon
on duty in the Philippines, simply went to the hospital and had
it out, in the widely touted belief that the vermiform appendix

was a useless vestige of some pre-Darwinian era. (Much later on I learned that the fashion was encouraged by professors of surgery to give youngsters lots of harmless practice, since even tonsillectomies could involve tampering with beds of white blood cells.)

However, since Watergate ours has become the age of the resurrected muckraker. And no sooner had the surgeon supplanted Dr. Kildare and Marcus Welby as Everyman's medical demigod than a new television series appeared designed to debunk the soaring reputation of the crack surgeon. It is called *Medical Story*. It has an authoritative air because it possesses the novelty of being impressively technical. Perhaps too technical. For forty years or more motion-picture audiences, seeing a young woman go suddenly into labor, have been trained almost to join the rural doctor in his cry for "lots of hot water." And television audiences are accustomed, once or twice a week, to hear men in masks demand a scalpel. But in *Medical Story* they are required in a trice to recognize a retractor and, in cases of severe heart attacks, to back the young resident against the old cardiologist in asking for a defibrillator.

The very first program exploited the recent survey that announced, on dubious statistical evidence, that one operation in five in the United States is unnecessary and that of these the great majority are hysterectomies. In this program a famous old surgeon performed a hysterectomy over the strenuous protest of the young resident that the woman's trouble was an endocrine disturbance. The woman died. The resident insisted on having his say in the review of the findings. The famous surgeon was censured and, in the interests of morale, the resident was fired for insubordination. But he went off at the end, like Charlie Chaplin ambling towards the horizon, a pathetic figure but definitely our hero still. In *Medical Story* first-year residents regularly challenge the diagnoses and the operative methods of senior surgeons. Indeed, the central thesis of *Medical Story* is that the young learners are thoughtful and humane, while the old experts are arrogant and fallible.

Well, you will be delighted to hear, *Medical Story* doesn't appear to be doing very well. Because, I believe, most people don't want to hear that surgeons are fallible. It's bad enough knowing that businessmen go broke, and lawyers lose cases, and politicians fail to govern. But when the layman has need of a surgeon he desperately wants to believe that he is the best in the world. (If things turn out a little rough there's always the consolation of a malpractice suit. But that's your worry, not his.)

And if in doubt he prefers an older hero to a younger one. I realize that I may be speaking only for my own generation. For it has been my observation that the layman, in all arcane matters—and especially in the mysteries having to do with health and disease—tends to run with his own generation. The young in America, as much as anywhere else, are quick to suspect the credentials of the middle-aged. Since, like the rest of us, they mix with their own, it is from them that they hear the wonders of the latest drugs, the ingenuities of new surgical techniques. My generation, on the contrary, assumes that a young doctor, however eminent he may come to be, hasn't yet seen enough variations of a clinical condition to know how wide and eccentric is a true definition of the normal.

I should like to believe that sensible doctors of any age would sooner than later say "Amen" to a great passage of William James. It is this:

> We become authorities and experts in the practical and scientific spheres by so many separate acts and hours of work. If anyone keeps faithfully busy each hour of the working day, he may safely leave the final result to itself. He can with perfect certainty count on waking up some fine morning to find himself one of the competent ones of

his generation . . . silently, between all the details of his business, "the power of judging" . . . will have built itself up within him.

Here is comfort for the old in the remembrance of their experiences, good and bad, and consolation for the young in the daily drudgery that takes so long to turn knowledge into wisdom. I am convinced that the only thing a man of fifty knows that a man of twenty does not, both of them being equally endowed, has nothing to do with an accumulation of knowledge: it has to do with guessing a little more certainly how human beings are likely to act. With surgeons, how the body *and* the human being are likely to behave.

I do believe this. And while nobody should preen himself, as long as he draws breath, that he *has* "the power of judging," it seems to me that, in any profession, the hints of that power that come occasionally to the young, and the proofs of it that come more frequently to the old, are what make worthwhile all those years in-between of keeping "faithfully busy each hour of the working day."

The State of the Language

GIVEN BEFORE AN ENGLISH SPEAKING UNION
CONFERENCE OF BRITISH AND AMERICAN SCHOLARS, IN
SAN FRANCISCO, NOVEMBER 1, 1979

The State of the Language

I apologize for taking out a script. I am in the habit, myself—especially after dinner—of speaking off the cuff or the top of the head, according to which is more available at the time. But this is an occasion with a special hazard. I am facing a pack of linguistic watchdogs who, like the people who review anthologies, are not going to be impressed by a wealth of accurate knowledge (even if I had it) so much as by small omissions and single slips.

As when J. B. Sykes put out, after seven years of lonely labor, his monumental new *Concise Oxford Dictionary* (a small monument but an exquisite one), one London reviewer spent little time applauding the thousands of definitions that are miracles of clarity and exactness. He took up most of his column protesting the secondary definition given to a simple four-letter word that, Sykes said, was a slang term of abuse applied usually to a woman. Not so, said the reviewer, and he went on and on about Sykes's insensitivity to pejorative usage in general and this cutting example in particular. I blush, even in this year of liberation, to pronounce the word. I leave you to rush home, get out your Sykes, and—beginning with the letter A—keep going till you find it.

I am told that the coming seminars will be addressed by

experts in Legal English and Black English, in everything from the new Episcopalian liturgy to the new liturgy of copulation. I am honored to be invited to kick off this series of matches between the structuralists and the semanticists and the other fashionable combatants. Fifty years ago, I might have had something special to offer, for it was a time when I sat at the feet of Dr. Richards trying to fathom the Meaning of Meaning, and when his most precocious pupil, William Empson, was warning us that nothing is as simple as it seems or sounds. But I have strayed very far from those battles long ago, and my effort this evening is so humble that it may affront many people here. It has to do with the state of the language as it is being used in the day-to-day intercourse of people: of politicians and voters, of advertisers and consumers, of businessmen and customers, of broadcasters and their listeners, of you and me going about the ordinary business of life.

A generation ago, I should have said that I was making a plea to everyone who works with children to see that they get a grounding in English grammar and English idiom, and pay particular attention to such things as the great range of connectives, like "on the whole" and "yet" and "for that matter"; and see that they become familiar with the wonderful economical uses of such words as we rarely hear in the Congress of the United States: "by," "with," "from," "about," "so," "because."

Today, I'm afraid, this plea must be extended not only to people who work with children but with high school pupils, with undergraduates, not least with Ph.D.s. A distinguished professor of English gave me the cue, in saying, "We take for granted that our students, certainly our graduate students, have a grasp of literate idiomatic English. But I find that only two or three of them can handle with any confidence straightforward declarative sentences, let alone subsidiary clauses."

In any given year, I get several thousand letters, and among them are letters from simple folk over sixty years of age who begin by apologizing for their ineptness with the language. They then write short, straightforward, clear, and surprisingly ept letters. On the contrary, the letters I get from graduate students (especially if they are in something called Creative Writing), from businessmen, even from some university presidents, most of all from politicians—are so barnacled with jargon that they bruise the wastebasket as they fall into it. Most of their sentences start with a foggy abstract noun, which in English locks you at once into the passive voice and traps you (as any meteorologist will tell you) into building one cumulus cloud on another, until the simple knowledge of who is doing what to whom is hidden from view.

I shan't bore or detain you—for the time it would take— by reciting the two sentences of Lincoln's tough stand on the relation of the Negroes' freedom to the Civil War as they would have been written today by a presidential candidate or his ghost writer. The original went like this: "If I could save the Union without freeing any slave, I would do it; and if I could save it by freeing all the slaves, I would do it; and if I could save it by freeing some and leaving others alone, I would also do that. The thing is to save the Union."

Senator Kennedy told us recently that, like Wendy Hiller, he knows where he's going. He didn't say that. He said: "I am not—er—unmindful of the—er—direction in which I am moving." If Lincoln were alive today, he would cut like a machete through the jungle of presidential double-talk. Why do they do it? The answer I believe is that sometime between childhood and middle age, they were brainwashed out of the early simplicities of their schooldays by advertising English and corporation English and federal prose. How otherwise does it come about that a Secretary of State, wanting to say that Spain needed money from us and needed it soon, could say: "That country's economic requirements from us should be given the highest priority in the shortest possible time frame"? How can we put ourselves at the mortal mercy of a Secretary of Defense who said the other day, about the President's decision to swash a buckle or two in Cuba: "What we are doing are [*sic*] reminders . . . and increases the downstrike capability"? How can a man who gets to be an emcee on a national network stop a woman from blabbing out a name by warning her: "We don't want to name any specific individual by name"? (Question: what is a nonspecific individual?)

Well, these people are in their forties, or fifties, or sixties and so are beyond redemption. They are not suddenly going to start talking like John Bunyan, or Defoe, or Lincoln, or Art Buchwald. I am thinking rather of the millions of schoolchildren who might yet be saved. Children to whom a television set is, in a literal sense, more impressive than any teacher they hear in a classroom. Who is to train them in the splendid flexibility of English tenses? Who is going to get them used to saying "because" instead of "in view of the fact that"? Who is to warn them that "in terms of" is usually a way of vamping till you're ready to think? Who is to give them warning signals about the whole Grammar of Anxiety, which springs from the chronic fear of being thought uneducated or banal and coins such things as "more importantly," "he invited Mary and I," "when I was first introduced," and "the end result"? Is anybody, in any high school in this country or in Britain, doing—under the lively influence of old Quiller-Couch and the Fowler brothers—what was done to me: giving out every so often a list of vogue words, and buzzwords, and current jargon, which you must translate into simple English and so need never use? If this had happened soon enough, and was a standard routine of early education, we should now have politicians who'd tell us what they have in mind, instead of which "scenarios" they are in the process of "orchestrating."

I have an English friend, the chairman of an advertising firm, who had the luck to go, forty-some years ago, to an English elementary school. Otherwise, he might be considered (as an advertising man) a kind of genius. For he is proof against genteelisms, circumlocutions, and general pomp. A few months ago, he sent a memo to his copywriters. It said: "On their way across the Atlantic are one or two pernicious buzzwords. The latest have been invented by theatre critics, but you might be tempted to pick them up and apply them to some product or fashion model. An actor is now said to give a 'resonant' performance. The movie critics have just discovered that the chief virtue of every sympathetic actress is that she is 'vulnerable.' I also caught one of you last week using the most meaningless word in the language—'meaningful.' Wake up, beware!"

What is the point of sending promising students (what in America we call "very bright" students) running after courses in Creative Writing when they haven't learned to walk with simple adverbs and prepositions? There is surely no point whatever in setting up a course in the works of S. J. Perelman (which, since he has died, they will soon be doing) for any student who has not acquired considerable sophistication in sensing the emotional tone—what you might call the secret public attitude—of various vocabularies from the Anglo-Saxon Chronicles to *Time,* from Thackeray to Erica Jong.

We are back with the impressionable child, who sits before the tube for several hours a day and gradually ceases to know that the words "early" and "late" are going from the language: Americans are either "ahead of schedule" or "behind schedule." No child today has heard of toothpaste. My grandson, at the age of three, babbled for his dentifrice. Long before he gets false teeth (or "dentures") he'll want some personal notepaper, but he'll have to ask for "personalized" notepaper. At the moment, his teacher tells us, he cannot be said to love football: he is "football-oriented." No American girl with cracked lips is told how to moisten them. She is handed a "moisturizer" by a mother who, no doubt, thinks of herself as nothing so square as a good parent but as a "supportive" or "caring" one, but doesn't care enough to stop her child imbibing from the telly, at a fearful daily rate, words, locutions, solecisms, and absurdities beyond the wit or attention of its teachers ever to correct. Children listen to the evening weather reports. They must be now inured to the fact (which may astonish some of our English visitors) that in the United States there is no longer any thunder, any rain, hail, or snow, and no clouds. There is only "thunderstorm activity" and "precipitation activity" and "cloud cover." A television weatherman told me the other evening that precipitation activity was spreading down from the Illinois area through the Kentucky and Tennessee areas into the Mississippi area. Poor Jack Teagarden! If he were alive today, he would have to sing "Stars Fell on the Alabama Area."

"Area" is my all-time nonfavorite: a cloudy word that has blanketed, and hence obliterated, the differences between neighborhood, district, part of town, region, state, field (of study), topic, theme. Airplanes used to stop at the gate. Now they "make a complete stop at the gate area." From which you proceed to the baggage claim area, and on into the New York or Dallas or San Francisco area. I once asked a skittish and amiable stewardess—or "in-flight hostess"—"How is it possible to be approaching the San Francisco area without approaching San Francisco?" She looked alarmed. "Search me," she said. My theory is simple, if revolutionary. There is an area of the United States that was named Illinois. There's another called New York, and yet another called Boston. However much they expand, that is what they should be called. When the time comes, I should be happy if they chiseled on my gravestone: "He killed off area."

I used to think that Americans were much better informed than Britons about medicine. Because they used, with enviable flipness, exact medical terms like "deviated septum" or "congested sinuses," whereas Britons tended to go round grumbling about their catarrh (catarrh in my day covered everything from pneumonia to a brain tumor). I remember becoming so ashamed of my lumpish ignorance of such things that I stopped talking about my lumbago (or rheumatics) and learned to toss off words like "sacroiliac" and "slipped disk" (even after an orthopedic surgeon asked me what I meant by it). It took some years for me to discover that the ordinary American, the layman, was no more knowledgeable than his British counterpart. He simply yielded to the national love of Latin and Greek (especially if he knew no Latin or Greek). Thus, I was enormously impressed when I heard somebody say, at a cocktail party, that he'd suffered a lesion of—or to—his clavicle. I tiptoed off to the dictionary to learn about this exotic affliction. What d'you think? He'd hurt his collarbone!

It used to be—and I'd like to think it's still so in some English-speaking countries—that when you had a pain and went to the doctor, a friend would say: "What did he do for you?" And you'd say: "He gave me a pill." No longer, not in this country. You are given "medication" and are not being treated: you are undergoing "therapy" ("treatment" in Greek). Chemotherapy, which means no more than treatment by a chemical, is now so exclusively applied to cancer that it seems cruel to remark that almost everything you put in your mouth, from an aspirin to a hamburger, is a chemical.

Another medical word that is very popular in America, and has been, I should guess, for a couple of decades, is the magic word "virus." All suffering people drop it to explain everything from a sniffle to a drowsiness. I used to drop it myself till a doctor present said thoughtfully: "I don't *think* it's a virus. I doubt it has protein coat." That's a stopper if ever I heard one. I looked that up too, and I'm ready anytime for any pedant who fixes me with his Ancient Mariner eye and says: "Do you know exactly what a virus *is?*" I reply at once: "Sure thing. Any of numerous kinds of very simple organisms smaller than bacteria, mainly of nucleic acid in protein coat, existing only in living cells and able to cause diseases." *That* shuts them up, even though I wouldn't know a nucleic acid if it were served to me chilled, with an olive, in a glass.

Some years ago, when I was traveling all over the country filming my television series *America,* one of the young women on the crew, a shrewd, modest English girl, who had not been here before, said: "They are a marvelous warm people, and their slang is so racy. But why is it that in print, or in public, the rule seems to be: 'Never say in two syllables what you can say in five'? Where did it all start?"

Well, there are two "its" here: the obsessive love of Latinisms; and the disastrous decline in the teaching of elementary grammar and plain speaking. I suspect that the early warning signal of a coming influx of polysyllables was the decision (I think in Goethe's time) by the University of Göttingen to begin and maintain a close relation with Harvard. It was enough, after the liberal revolution of 1848, and more than enough in the later trek of German exiles, to guarantee invading hordes of sociologists and psychiatrists. It has become a badge, almost a sworn oath, of their trade that it is better to be overwrought than oversimple; that Anglo-Saxon English is a naive tool for examining human behavior either in the individual or in the mass; that the love of a man for a maid is not to be undertaken lightly, but gravely, writhingly, humorlessly, pedantically, as a perilous adventure in "interpersonal relationships."

As for the decline in teaching grammar, in some schools the deliberate abandoning of it, I believe it started when John Dewey conceived the beguiling theory that all knowledge can be "fun," if not orgasmic. The application of this theory far and wide by slaphappy people who thought of themselves as "progressives" led in the fullness of time to a masterpiece of wishful thinking that I saw enshrined in a newspaper ad at the end of last March. It said: "You Can Learn French by the 15th of

May—*with no effort on your part!"* I thought of Charles Darwin, going down to various seashores on and off for over forty years with a broken teacup (he had no grant from a national science foundation) and scooping up sand and algae and brooding over them. At the end of which time, after considerable effort on his part, he published *The Origin of Species.* But then, Darwin was a Victorian, and he held to the Victorian prejudice that any knowledge that goes much below the surface takes time and tedium to acquire—however "bright" the student.

Some years ago, I was saying much of this—as it applied to the jargon of medicine—to the assembled staff of the Mayo Clinic. I mused that perhaps, after all, an appetite for jargon might be imbibed with the mother's milk: a matter of genes. I was rash enough to conclude: "Maybe you can no more cure a naturally pompous person than you can reflower a virgin." My lecture was reprinted in the *Mayo Clinic Bulletin,* which goes to the far corners of the earth. One of the first letters I received was from the University of Tokyo's department of gynecology. It said: "But, Mr. Cooke, we do it!"

If they can do it, maybe our high school teachers can make it unnecessary, by encouraging and training the child's instinct for directness and simplicity before the hymen, so to speak, of its innocence is broken. At any rate, I'm convinced that it is in the high schools at the latest that the old custom should be revived: the teaching, first, of grammar and idiom; and then, of cautionary courses in current jargon. The time to rinse the mind free of verbal cant cannot begin too early.

I trust that "the development of this basic linguistic concept mandates no further elaboration at this point in time." Or, as Chaucer more aptly put it, "there is no more to saye." Except, thank you and—"Have a nice day in the San Francisco area."

Freedom and the Soldier

GIVEN AT THE UNITED STATES MILITARY ACADEMY, WEST
POINT, FEBRUARY 19, 1980

Freedom and the Soldier

First, let me say that it is a privilege to be invited to talk to you about a word that has only to be pronounced to imply the threat of its opposite: "tyranny." And so, in a flash, it summons up for us the two main types of society that have always been in opposition, and very often at war, during the past three hundred years. The scriptures of the American Revolution—the Declaration, the pamphlets, the broadsides, the public proclamations, the songs—use the word "liberty" like a drumbeat. And since the Revolution was a success, Americans came to believe that they had a proprietary hold on the word and what it stood for. This proud delusion—that the United States is the first or only fountain of freedom—is still maintained, indeed resoundingly advertised during presidential campaigns. So that people who ought to know better, who might be expected to have some rude knowledge of the parliamentary systems of Europe, of India, of Australasia, regularly proclaim the United States to be the one and only true home of freedom.

In your lifetime, the word has become a buzzword, like "establishment," "fascist," "liberal," "conservative," "reactionary." It is a word passionately invoked by politicians, fuzzily distorted by every special interest, claimed as a registered patent by buccaneering businessmen, asserted as an unqualified right by leftists, sentimentalists, and pornographers, freely used by everybody, and defined by very few.

Your Superintendent courteously assured me that I was not obliged to talk about soldiers and soldiering. But I took this as a rare opportunity to do just that, because no profession confronts so often as yours must the contradiction between freedom and duty. Have no fear that I am about to indulge what, in this country as much as in any, is a favorite pastime of civilian commentators: telling the military where it went wrong. Although in a democracy we keep to the famous and sensible belief that war is too important to be left to the generals, I have seen enough of civilians running policy in wartime to know that nobody is more bloodthirsty, more exhilarated by the war game, than presidential assistants who are new to it. They give force to a warning maxim I have quoted before and will quote again: C. E. Montague's celebrated line "Hell hath no fury like a noncombatant scorned."

On the other hand, I recall that it was *General* William Tecumseh Sherman who said, "War is sheer barbarism." It was *General* Douglas MacArthur who begged both Presidents Kennedy and Johnson not to commit American forces to the Asian mainland and who, at the end of his life, said: "I am a one hundred percent disbeliever in war." It was *General* Dwight D. Eisenhower who, before any civilian, foresaw the new and dangerous relationship that technology would forge between the civilian and the soldier: "In the councils of government, we must guard against the acquisition of unwarranted influence, whether sought or unsought, by the military-industrial complex."

My military qualifications for talking on this topic at all are humble, not to say comical. But to recite them is enough to remind us how longingly civilian governments, when they choose to distribute honors, cling to the trappings of military pomp. For instance: I am a Kentucky Colonel, personally sworn by the Secretary of State of the Commonwealth of Kentucky to leap to the defense of its borders at the first whiff of an invader. I am also a Knight Commander of the British Empire, pledged to defend any threatened part of the Empire, provided somebody succeeds in putting it back on the map.

But, as a citizen of this country, and not less of the shrinking world we call free, and as one whose memory of great wars goes back to 1914, I hope my credentials are more legitimate. I was born in Lancashire, the kingdom of the Red Rose, as Yorkshire was the kingdom of the White Rose. And although when I was a boy the Wars of the Roses had been over for more than four hundred years (after Henry the Seventh got on the throne—a Lancastrian, I am happy to say), I was nevertheless brought up in the almost religious belief that all Englishmen were and ought to be free, except Yorkshiremen.

As a boy, I saw the Lancashire regiments go off from the Manchester railroad stations to France and remote theaters and saw maybe a half of them come back. Then came the peace, and famine among the ravaged countries of Europe. And I went to college and had the luck—as a very nonpolitical person—to interrupt the long Cambridge honeymoon with a spell of teaching school in Germany. There, in Munich, I once listened to a speech by a rabble-rouser whom nobody on the outside was paying much attention to. But I found myself, like the rest of the small outdoor audience, hypnotized by this powerful and subtle man. His name was Adolf Hitler.

In Dresden, I was taken to a restaurant and the waiter, against the manager's instructions, seated us at a table by the window. At the first appearance of a plate of soup, children tottered along from nowhere and glared through the window: small children with black circles under their eyes, ribcages as well defined as in an X-ray, and bellies swollen like balloons. Then the cops came swarming and beat them off. Back at school in Silesia, I was surrounded by country people so ground down by depression and hunger, and the vengeful conditions imposed on them by the Allies, that the best they could do was to scrape for food and dream of the dignity of a job and a halfway decent home. It would have been an insult to the facts of their life to talk to them about such rosy abstractions as civil rights or freedom. Survival was all. Then came Hitler, pointing to two scapegoat villains. He told them they were a fine, upstanding people cheated by the Allies and gouged by the Jews. And in relief and thanksgiving they rallied to him. Some of the German schoolmasters I knew went underground politically, and one or two of them later—God knows—literally. It was my first political lesson in the frailty of freedom. "No amount of political freedom," wrote Lenin, one month before the Russian Revolution, "will satisfy the hungry masses."

It is a sentence worth remembering whenever you come on the unemployment statistics, or consider that in the black slums of America one boy in two between the ages of fifteen and twenty-two not only has no job but has only the remotest prospect of one in his foreseeable future. To him, freedom is a luxury cruise on the other side of a pay envelope. When there are enough of him, of any race, and when their primary needs go unheeded, a free society is in trouble. It will erupt into disorder and social chaos (as Germany did), which will be pacified only by the arrival of a leader who suspends the laws and imposes his own. (I never believed that America was given freedom by act of God. And when Senator Joseph McCarthy, in the early fifties, was hounding everybody—including the army—for beliefs which—on paper-thin evidence—they were alleged to hold, I thought we were very fortunate not to have, as we'd had twenty years earlier, thirteen million unemployed. He might have torn up the Constitution.)

When a free society is hit by depression, and/or by uncontrollable inflation, no citizen is confronted by such an ordeal of conscience as the soldier. Is he committed to restore a kind of order that accords with his belief in freedom, or is he sworn to restore order *at all costs?* Does he obey his principles or the Fuehrer? I met Prussian officers of the best type who, finding this dilemma too uncomfortable to live with, retreated into the technicalities of their profession, cut themselves off from the nation that had been bullied into submission, and kept up their morale by privately despising Hitler and all his works. Some of the more philosophical of them did this, I'm sure, not out of cowardice but out of the professional conviction that Herman Melville's Captain Vere expressed to the naval court: "In receiving our commissions we in the most important regard ceased to be natural free agents . . . . we fight at command. If our judgments approve the war, that is but coincidence." It is a tragic dilemma that has plagued soldiers ancient and modern, from Brutus to Billy Budd's commander, from Billy Mitchell to Erwin Rommel.

I should guess that even in peacetime, and in times of what the Founding Fathers called "domestic tranquillity," one of the psychological hazards of being a soldier is nothing less than the social condition of the soldier's life: the sense of being isolated from the society you are pledged to defend. You are not entirely alone in this. To a lawyer everybody—including a doctor—is a client. To a doctor everybody—including a lawyer—is a patient. But they do not live together in a compound outside the bounds of general society. However, you are also citizens, part of the mass of people. And I should like to see all military and naval and air force and marine academies recruit a regular roster of speakers from every walk of life, to keep you reminded of the varieties of freedom that people claim: businessmen, labor union leaders, welfare workers, hospital directors, lawyers, farmers, shopkeepers, longshoremen, drug rehabilitators, Congressmen, women's liberators, abortionists, anti-abortionists, nurses, engineers. Mainly, people who are in the thick of one job. To talk to you about their jobs and how they work, and fail to work. Even bankers of no general intelligence have one lobe of the brain that is expert in the moving or making of money, and it is worth probing.

If there is one thing I learned from thirty years as a foreign correspondent, roaming around every corner of this country, and talking one day with a Senator and then with a trucker, with a hospital orderly or a Mafia chieftain, with an oil expert in Oklahoma, a tattooist in San Diego, a sheep-sluicer in West Texas—I learned at first hand that no profession is as simple as it seems to an outsider, and that a free society is a great deal harder to run than an authoritarian one, if only because of the great range of opinion, prejudice, and self-interest, and the difficulty of disciplining these lively feelings in the general interest.

Time and again in our government, we see the votes in Congress decided not by a free judgment of the majority but by the successful pressure of a minority interest—that is, by the self-interest of a powerful lobby, which is yielded to because every Congressman hopes that next time he can get a majority vote for *his* favorite lobby. Some people deplore this as a new and dangerous tyranny, a tyranny of factions, of special interests. But James Madison, even before political parties were invented in this country, looked on the conflict of factions as a healthy sign, as indeed the essence, of representative government. He insisted only that there be plenty of different factions, attached to the interests of different parts of the country.

Of course, the most effective way to cut through the babel of competing voices and interests is to get strong executive leadership. And we hear a great deal today—and always in an election year—of the need, the hunger, for a strong leader. It is a mischievous longing. For it is one of the permanent contradictions of a democratic society that strong personal leadership is only possible during a war, when many democratic liberties (the First Amendment as an example) have to be suspended or greatly restricted.

I have not so far talked much about freedom as an abstract

idea but as something that applies to you in practice; rather, it must seem, as something that hardly applies to you, since you live in a closed society and have chosen at the start to abide by a system of rules and taboos that millions of Americans would regard as denials of freedom itself. That's only because, but it *is* because, we are living in a time when "freedom" is given a definition so boundless that a whole generation wallows in the notion that the First Amendment gives Americans a license to do anything they want, at any time, in any place. Or, at the very least to echo a famous English political leader when he said: "Real freedom means good wages, short hours, security in employment, good homes, opportunity for leisure and recreation with family and friends." That sounds like a universal prescription–what every politician—Republican, Communist, Liberal, Democrat, Socialist, Conservative—is offering us: what, indeed, television advertising is all about. I wonder if the applause for that sentence would die down if we revealed its author. He was Oswald Mosley announcing the true faith as the leader of the British Fascists. These promises have nothing to do with freedom. You can have "good wages, short hours, security in employment, good homes, opportunity for leisure and recreation with family and friends" in a nation in which a personal opinion, a dissenting speech, a disturbing scientific discovery, the booing of a public speaker, is a passport to exile, a labor camp, a prison, a psychiatric hospital, or a firing squad.

Freedom is a good deal more than general comfort. And much more demanding. It may be news to some people to hear that liberty demands anything. But, for one thing, it demands voluntary limits on freedom itself. Over eighty years ago, the greatest of American jurists, Mr. Justice Holmes, put his finger on the favorite maxim of many people who say, "I can do what I like provided it doesn't seem to hurt other people." "The liberty of the citizen," he wrote, "to do as he likes so long as he does not interfere with the liberty of others to do the same has [become] a shibboleth. . . . [But] it is interfered with by school laws, by the post office, by every state or municipal institution which takes his money for purposes thought desirable whether he likes it or not."

Justice Holmes was expressing this opinion at a time when nobody seriously questioned the sense or necessity of school laws or post office regulations or the need to be taxed to maintain state or municipal institutions. But there was then, as now, a popular rhetoric of freedom that blinds otherwise intelligent people to the distinction between those parts of life that have to do with freedom and the parts that don't. Well into this century, it was taken for granted that a doctor or a policeman or a fireman would always be on hand. When the police of Boston—following the example of the police of London and Liverpool—organized in a union in order to press as a body for decent wages, they astounded the nation by going on strike. There was a very ugly twenty-four-hour bout of looting, and the army was called in. When the president of the American Federation of Labor asked that the police be returned to their jobs, the governor of Massachusetts refused and made an announcement which to the rest of the country had the force of holy writ: "There is no right to strike against the public safety by anybody, anywhere, anytime." This recital of the obvious brought him a wire of congratulation from President Wilson and, the next year, the vice-presidential nomination of his party, and, two years later (by the grace of God's disposal of Warren Harding), the presidency.

I don't think today it would bring him anything but defiance and uproar. In Coolidge's time, society had the positive restraints of institutional religion, and the negative restraints of what most people thought unthinkable. Together these checks disciplined, or at worst cowed, the vast majority of people into socially acceptable behavior.

Today, religion has lost its restraining power, even in predominantly religious nations; obedience to constituted authority is widely confused with authoritarianism; and almost anything is thinkable, including frequent assertions of the rights of citizenship which implicitly deny that it carries any duties at all (such as, for instance, being counted in the census or submitting to registration for military service).

A week or more ago, there was a parade in Princeton of young protesters against the idea not of a draft but of draft registration. One sign carried the slogan "There Is Nothing Worth Dying For." That seems to me to be the witless end of Know-Nothingism. If enough Americans felt that way, this nation would long ago have succumbed to a dictatorship.

But this, too, is nothing new. It is a feeling that disrupts most societies in the exhaustion of a long war. We had our draft riots during the Civil War, race riots during the Second World War, and an unprecedented outcry against the war in Vietnam. In the middle 1930s, the memory of the enormous slaughter of the First World War was still so green that when Hitler went on the rampage, the prospect of war actually stimulated, in millions of Europeans, a longing for peace at any price. This disillusion suppressed the recognition that some things have to be fought for—so much so, that there was a powerful and popular slogan which helped Britain put its head in the sand. It was "Against War and Fascism," a cry about as sensible as "Against Hospitals and Disease." It was chanted most fervently by people who were willing to do absolutely anything to get rid of Hitler, except fight him. This muddled thinking persisted until it was almost too late. Munich may have been—as Churchill said at the time—"a total and unmitigated defeat." But the popular mood had impressed itself on the Conservative government in the form of believing that if you don't rearm you won't have to fight. So Munich became a longed-for surrender. It was also,

I'm afraid, a necessary one. Britain did not have the power to protect the freedom of Czechoslovakia, or its own. London had two antiaircraft guns.

Well, it will be no news to you that your profession is not popular. It rarely has been in the United States. Today, it is a profession especially despised by morally superior people, whose sense of moral superiority is, in fact, made possible by your existence. We, the United States, are today one of the few free nations that do not have a system of military conscription. And yet the volunteer army is not working, because there aren't enough volunteers. And the chief of naval operations recently confided to the Joint Chiefs of Staff that the poor pay of skilled petty officers is stripping the navy of the men it needs to run its ships.*

I am not advocating military conscription. I am saying that the lack of it is not a sign of our superior freedom, only of our superior optimism. Or maybe the very general feeling that since the Soviet and American acquisition of the nuclear bomb and the well-publicized stalemate of a "balance of terror," a conventional war would be impossible, in spite of the glaring fact that—precisely because the use of the bomb is unthinkable—there have been more conventional wars in the past quarter-century (about 120 at the last count) than in all of the nineteenth century.

I think, too, that our strong resistance to any compulsory service proposed by the national government is a sharp reflection of what I believe to be our striking preference for equality over liberty: if all men are created equal, then I'm just as good as you, whoever you are, and probably better. At any rate, I should

---

*Four years after this speech was given, the volunteer system began to work very well indeed, after a legislated increase in pay. But the new recruits are still preponderantly found among the poor and the unskilled.

not like to see the results of a national survey of honest opinion about whether we cherish liberty more than equality, or *comfort* more than either. It was a very comfortable, a self-indulgent and wealthy, author, Somerset Maugham, who saw the French refugees—rich and poor—trudging the roads in flight from the oncoming Nazis (who were on their way, no doubt, to his own luxurious villa in the south of France). He found himself saying something that most of his readers would not have expected from his lips: "If a nation values anything more than freedom, it will lose its freedom; and the irony of it is that if it is comfort or money that it values more, it will lose that too."

So—in our time, when we see comfort, and anarchy, and even violence, being claimed as expressions of freedom, and when many peaceable and well-meaning people seem unaware that individual liberty has its limits, what is the effective form of social discipline? Plainly, it is no longer church or even appeals to the sanctity of the law. The only safeguard, as I see it, is the safeguard of what most people *feel they ought not to do.* I have said this elsewhere, and I repeat it here without apology, because I cannot say it any better:

> As for the rage to believe that we have found the secret of liberty in general permissiveness from the cradle on, this seems to me to be a disastrous sentimentality, which, whatever liberties it sets loose, loosens also the cement that alone can bind any society into a stable compound—a code of obeyed taboos. I can only recall the saying of a wise Frenchman that "liberty is the luxury of self-discipline." Historically those peoples that did not discipline themselves had discipline thrust on them from the outside. That is why the normal cycle in the life and death of great nations has been: first, a powerful tyranny, broken by revolt, then the enjoyment of liberty, then the abuse of liberty—and back to tyranny again. As I see it, in this country—a land

of the most persistent idealism and the blandest cynicism—
the race is on between its decadence and its vitality.*

To come back to the ordeal of the Prussian officers under
Hitler, ultimately what matters is not how you look to the
administration or to your classmates. It matters how, if you are
religious, you look to your Maker. If you are not religious, how
you look to your conscience, which is the seedbed of honor, a
word very rarely used by honorable people, who tend to stay
mum on Emerson's sound principle: "The louder he talked of
his honor, the faster we counted our spoons."

I do not fool myself that everybody here joined the army
in order to defend liberty. Every profession has its morbid at-
tractions. Think of the surgeon who has found a socially sanc-
tioned exercise in sadism. The social scientist who has found a
quick formula for becoming a know-all. You have all, I hope,
learned how often—how almost automatically—in many countries of South and Central America the army is the obvious
weapon to call on when you want to stifle freedom as quickly
as possible.

But to the extent that you here are ready to sacrifice the
easy life to defend not what is craven or greedy or brutal or
muddled about our society but what is free and humane about
it: ladies and gentlemen, I salute you.

America, p. 388.

Doctor and Patient: Face to Face

KEYNOTE ADDRESS GIVEN AT THE BRITISH MEDICAL
ASSOCIATION CONGRESS, SAN DIEGO, CALIFORNIA,
OCTOBER 19, 1981

Doctor and Patient:
Face to Face

W hat I have in mind is the daily relation of the doctor (most especially the internist or general practitioner) to the patients he sees, and the cures or placebos he offers them. Most of all I want to address myself to the psychological assumptions on which both doctor and patient gauge each other's character and temperament and adjust their attitudes accordingly. If I have anything to offer to doctors, who have spent their lifetimes with this problem, it may be to sharpen some of the differences that I have noticed, in Britain and America, between what the doctor expects of the patient and what the patient expects of the doctor.

Some of you may be disappointed to infer—correctly—that I am not going to discuss the big social themes that have been well aired by people far more knowledgeable than I: such things as the proper distribution of rural and city doctors, and profit-making private clinics; let alone the large and universal problems of socialized medicine versus private practice, and the never-ending arguments that flow from a national health insurance system about how thorough a clinical routine can be applied to a horde of people in the waiting room who are there because the service is free. I will only say in passing that very few people I have ever heard of are willing to put money aside for health insurance. All systems so-called would be better labeled sickness-insurance programs.

One of the sharpest differences between Britain and America is how much the doctor expects the patient to know about the working of his body in general and the particular troubles he is susceptible to. Nobody has written more aptly about this—as about many other relations between doctors and patients—than the late Richard Asher. At your annual meeting twenty-two years ago, he said: "Indirectly, a little knowledge of medicine in the hands of our patients may benefit doctors. It is hard for a salesman to remain honest if his customers have no idea whether his goods are satisfactory or not. Blind, ignorant faith in doctors is not always to their benefit, although we appreciate it highly on the rare occasions we obtain it. Heaven defend us from the kind of patient who comes to us and says: 'I want you to have my 17-keto-steroids estimated.' How much we prefer the patient who says: 'I leave it to you, doctor.' "

I am sure that while these two types stake out the extremes of the general practitioner's experience, there are many more varied types in between—suppliants, admirers, doubting Thomases, paranoiacs, pests. The technically inquisitive patient is, I suspect, far more common in the United States. In my frequent shuttling between the two countries, I have often thought that British doctors are lucky in having, in their educated patients especially, an ignorant laity that would rather remain so. This must have something to do with the persistence in Britain of C. P. Snow's two cultures, which encourage the automatic decision among university students to go into the arts or sciences on the presumption that the twain are never meant to meet, and with the general presumption of writers, lawyers, musicians, artists that no intellectual or social prestige is lost by regarding the sciences as beneath their notice. In glaring contrast to this national prejudice, I think of the not unusual American career of the late Robert Tyre Jones, Jr., of Atlanta, Georgia. If he had been an

Englishman, I doubt whether before he became the greatest golfer in the world he would have acquired an honors degree in English literature from Oxford, a law degree from the Middle Temple, and an engineering degree from Manchester.

I find that in even the most distinguished British biographies of literary figures, musicians, and artists, five hundred pages of the most scrupulous scholarship will end with the note that the great man or woman tired easily, was in increasing pain, and friends knew that "the end was near." Nearly fifty years ago my first American friend, who was then a premedical student at Yale, on coming to the end of a biography of some eighteenth-century writer (it could just as well have been a twentieth-century figure) said: "What *is* this listlessness that killed him? Was it an anemia, diabetes, encephalitis, or what?" An annoyingly large number of Americans, from all sorts of backgrounds, tend to want to know. And so the American internist expects to be burdened by this nagging demand—from a lawyer, a housewife, an actor, or a real estate broker—for a technical explanation that would bore or bewilder the more stoical Briton.

American curiosity is fed daily at high and low levels. At the lowest it is fed by the preposterous magical cures propounded by weekly junk magazines that litter the display shelves of supermarkets. At the highest level it is fed by television documentaries and by the excellent and wide-ranging articles on health and disease that appear in the best of the American press. In how many other countries, I wonder, is a weekly scientific supplement enclosed in the daily newspaper, as it is every Tuesday in *The New York Times*?

As for television, it is at once a curse and a blessing. The curse is television commercials, from which viewers pick up, subliminally, in the moment of ridicule, quick fixes for indigestion, headaches, hemorrhoids, lower backache, insomnia, and what is guardedly called "minor arthritis pain." The blessing, not unmixed, lies in the frequent television documentaries on how the body works and how it doesn't. Here again, it is the nature of the medium to be most engrossing when it is most visually dramatic. Few inquisitive people can resist the marvelous world revealed to us by microphotography, and the most memorable medical documentaries I have seen have been of performances of microsurgery. Inevitably, these deal with impaired function which, without the intervention of the skilled surgeon, would kill the patient. Before television, something of the sort was done by documentary-film makers. I remember how enthusiastically, before the last war, the Roosevelt administration discovered the virtues, or rather the propaganda uses, of documentary film. One of the ablest of the directors hired by the government did a film called *The Birth of a Baby*. It was quite brilliant and received ecstatic reviews from everybody but—I should guess—expectant mothers. Throughout the film the heartbeat was amplified on the sound track and provided a relentless bass rhythm. The effect of it—as it pounded at a gallop and then perilously slowed—was ominous. For what the director was filming was not the normal birth of a baby but a terrifying case of eclampsia. It was, in other words, a film about disease. I should think it contributed powerfully to the abortion rate of the time—which was not its original purpose.

But the effects of television in general—its dramas, soap operas, its fictional life—go much further than most of us had guessed in implanting in the general public new attitudes towards the doctor. We have just learned this from a study conducted over the past ten years by the University of Pennsylvania. It is serious enough to merit its being published in full, later this year, by the United States Public Health Service. Its conclusions are at once flattering to the doctor and a threat to his honesty and patience. Here are the main ones:

Characters on evening prime-time serials are shown as healthy "despite all the mayhem, eating, and drinking" and are relatively sober, safe from accidents, and slim at all ages.

The image of mentally ill people presented by television fits erroneously into stereotypes and popular prejudice.

There are five times as many doctors, nurses, and other health professionals on television as there are in real life.

Daytime soap operas rely for their cliff-hanging tension on so much illness, major and minor, that "they could well be the largest source of medical advice in the United States."

These characteristics alone, by reinforcing the preconception that doctors are available in all places at all hours, could well make the patient who suddenly falls ill all the more outraged by the reality of the unreachable doctor and the tedium and trauma of the emergency clinic; they may have done much to stimulate what is called "roadside medicine" and the mushrooming growth of freestanding emergency centers, or walk-in clinics, with a promised limit of fifteen minutes' waiting time.

The most somber and threatening—threatening to you— sentence in the report is this one, which starts out as a seeming compliment: "Television contributes to a syndrome in which high levels of confidence in the medical profession seem to justify live-for-today attitudes. . . . This cultivation of complacency, coupled with an unrealistic belief in the 'magic of medicine,' is likely to perpetuate unhealthy life-styles and to leave both patients and doctors vulnerable to disappointment, frustration— and litigation."

Litigation! The dread word reminds us of the enormous increase in this country, in the past twenty years or so, of suits for malpractice, and a corresponding increase in protective premiums, so stiff in some states that there are skillful surgeons who have quit their practices and turned to more dependable ways of providing for their families.* It is taken, by many

---

*By 1985, of all medical specialists, obstetricians had become the most vulnerable to legal action. In some states, their annual malpractice insurance premiums were as high as $70,000, and as many as one in four were quitting their practices.

newspapers and other media, as a grisly reflection of rampant malpractice. And it may be that as people come to expect more from doctors, more doctors take bigger risks to accommodate them. But many of these suits reflect rather the bitter disillusion of a generation lulled by the popular education we have been talking about into believing that doctors can cure any disease, and that almost any organ of the body can be replaced as readily as a punctured tire or a shock absorber.

So one big social question that the modern doctor has to face is: who will help him adjust to these rosy expectations and regain the realistic confidence of his patients? Well, there is good news. The answer is—the sociologists, whose main job, after all, is to tell us how society works and, by the disinterestedness of their findings, point the way to its behaving better. In the past ten years the sociologists have turned their expertise to the doctor-patient relationship. The studies I have seen are based on the premise, which seems to me a sensible one, that the root of a trusting relationship or a suspicious one lies in the first interview. Consequently, they went out with microphones and tape recorders, in Southern and Northern California, in Washington, D.C., in Massachusetts, and in West Germany, to tape the dialogues between doctors and their new patients.

The reports I have looked over should not raise your hopes for enlightenment too high. They appear to me to share two initial flaws. The first is almost inevitable in a procedure that requires both the doctor and the patient to be told that they are going to be recorded. The happy injunction to "just be yourself" is one with which naive radio and television producers hope to comfort beginning broadcasters. The truth is that to ninety-nine human beings in a hundred, however emotionally secure or blithe they may be in life, a microphone is a sword of Damocles that instantly heightens self-consciousness and produces a tune (what the phoneticians call an "intonation pattern") which is not the natural tune of a person talking to one or two friends in a room—and that, to me, is the ideal condition for all successful broadcasting. It takes years to forget the microphone and any awareness of an outside audience.

So, in the transcripts of the interviews I have read there is an unnatural strain on both sides, which is in itself a source of suspicion. Many doctors seem to overcome this better than their patients, however, and this leads the recording angels—the sociologists—into their second flaw: the presumption, reported as an observation, that doctors tend, especially with less-educated patients, to be intimidating, to be exercising power. But surely the first meeting between a patient and a doctor, between the learner and the teacher, between the anxious ignoramus and the one who knows, cannot possibly be an equal emotional and psychological exchange.

Whatever else the sociologists can usefully tell us is befogged by their own appalling jargon. Let me recite—not for long—some of the discoveries which they seem to offer as being most relevant, if not profound.

They notice that patients develop an "attitude" to the doctor: "Specific aspects of the doctor's talk obviously contribute to this notion of attitude." The only comment I can make on that is: obviously. Some investigators, we are told, "use a scale of 1 to 6 to score . . . the least to the most technical remarks . . . [and] the same scale is used to decide the globality or specificity of the patient's questions and the doctor's responses. . . . additional scoring is used about the causal or noncausal nature of the explanation and its probabilistic or nonprobabilistic nature." Well, fancy that!

One original study "involved longitudinal observations of doctor-patient interaction between six internists and thirty-six patients over a nine-month period." What they were doing discussing longitude I have no idea, unless—as I can well imagine—the patients were so disoriented after nine months that they had to be told where they were at.

I am afraid there is no succor for us from the sociologists. I should like some doctors—neuropsychiatrists preferably—to do a study on the problems of communication that are peculiar to sociologists: why they fail to get anything at all across to poor us, their abject subjects.

Any of you frightened by these strictures may take decent consolation from the wiser words of Franz Ingelfinger, who four years ago, meeting the charge that doctors are more arrogant than most professionals, had this to say: "Physicians as a class are, I suspect, no more vain or insolent than any other people. Some are presumptuous and condescending, others self-effacing and sympathetic . . . [but] if the physician is to be effective in alleviating the patient's complaints, it follows that the patient has to believe . . . that his physician not only can be trusted but has also some special knowledge that the patient does not possess. He needs, if the treatment is to succeed, a physician whom he invests with authoritative experience and competence. He needs a physician from whom he will accept some domination. If I am going to give up eating eggs for the rest of my life, I must be convinced, as an ovophile, that a higher authority than I will influence my eating habits. I do not want to be in the position of the shopper at the casbah who negotiates and haggles with the physician about what is best. . . . In fact, if you agree that the physician's primary function is to make the patient feel better, a certain amount of authoritarianism, paternalism, and domination are the essence of the physician's effectiveness."

This must be so, though we have only to look around at any dozen, and apparently happy, marriages we know to see that for some people authority does not reside in domination but rather in the partner's serene temperament, or in humor, or in simply a pair of beautiful brown eyes. For me, medical authority is most acceptable in a doctor who is a skeptic.

I should like to end by considering briefly the special temptation that is offered by the present great age of biochemical medicine—the temptation to become what the late Dr. Haven Emerson called "the Ph.D.": the pharmacopoeia doctor, who listens to a recital of the symptoms, retires to the back room, matches the most distressing symptom with the latest drug, and prescribes it. The layman does not know that about a half of today's prescriptions are for drugs that did not exist ten years ago. With his preconceived trust in the doctor as a sainted healer, he is not disposed to discover that, according to a survey done as long ago as 1964, one in three prescriptions handed out by general practitioners is based on the information folders that come with the drug company's sample. Luckily for doctors, the time it takes for each succeeding wonder drug to be discredited, or restricted to its rare and proper use, is so long or so masked by gradual disuse that the disappointment or damage in the old drug is forgotten in the glowing promise of the new. I am thinking of those drugs which are seized on as God-sent solutions to ancient or particular problems and which, in time, reveal not so much that they have bad side effects but that the *effect on the ailments they are prescribed for may be the side effect,* the main effect being the damage done to some organ that was not considered in the original research or manufacture.

The example of thalidomide is too gross to enlarge on, although for a year or two its potential merit was seriously weighed and attested by some very competent physicians in the Western world. Those in active practice in the 1950s will recall chloramphenicol, a wonder drug indeed until it was seen to shut down the bone marrow. Those of us with any interest in athletics vividly recall the miracle we saw with our very eyes, when some football player received a brutal injury, limped or was carried off the field, and within ten minutes or so was trotting happily back into combat after a massive shot of hydrocortisone. We never noticed how many of these heroes went off into early retirement. More recently, phenylbutazone (Butazolidin) has been joyfully prescribed as the most magical of the anti-inflammatory drugs. Crippling muscle spasms vanish overnight! No wonder: as one orthopedic surgeon put it: "It's like killing a gnat with an atom bomb." And to this day, it takes courage for the good doctor to refuse to pump penicillin into patients with self-limiting ailments such as the common cold. The belief in fashionable magic has come so far in the United States that there are rich people, from Palm Beach to Beverly Hills, who at the onset of a headache demand a computed axial tomography (CAT) scan.*

As for the vitamins—apart from the weekly shots of vitamin B_{12} given patients who feel out of sorts but could not possibly have pernicious anemia—all but the most cynical doctors can be excused from blame, since vitamins constitute the most flourishing branch of the self-medication industry. First it was C, then the B complex, and now—in the United States—the magical E. I once tried to tell a devoted addict of vitamin E how Evans and Emerson, so long ago as 1936, labored to find for rats a diet deficient in vitamin E; how difficult this effort was; how the thing seemed to exist in cardboard, ground glass, and dust; how in the end those two pioneers isolated such a diet, so deficient in everything that the rats grew lackadaisical and some developed muscular dystrophy. Moreover, Mr. Rat was no longer interested in Mrs. Rat. *That* was the detail that excited the industry and the laggard lover. If you took lots of vitamin E surely your potency would be enhanced. It followed, did it not? It did not. But it was useless to suggest to my addict that the logic in this inference was about as sensible as deducing that if Neville Chamberlain had gone to Munich *without his umbrella* he would not have appeased Hitler. In fact, I believe that nothing at all can be done for patients, or nonpatients, who believe that with vitamins, more is better.

---

*Once the word gets around such chic environs that magnetic resonance imaging (MRI) could eventually replace both CAT scans and X rays, the MRI procedure may become as obligatory as access to a sauna.

But as I travel from place to place and country to country, I am constantly struck by finding that this friend in London, and that one in Dallas, another in Paris, and yet another in Glasgow are all getting the same, the latest, antibiotic though their ailments seem to be different. My conclusion is that, because this is an era of intensifying specialization and widespread biochemical experiment, there never was a time when the ordinary doctor, the general practitioner, needed to do more homework, to exercise more patience, and to direct his own and his patients' attention to the human body's subtle, and, indeed, preponderant capacity for *health*. Lewis Thomas has said it as well as anyone:

> It is a distortion . . . to picture the human being as a teetering, fallible contraption, always needing watching and patching, always on the verge of flapping to pieces; this is the doctrine that people hear most often, and most eloquently, on all our information media. We ought to be developing a much better system of general education about human health, with more curricular time for acknowledgment, and even some celebration, of the absolute marvel of good health that is the real lot of most of us, most of the time.

Well, I seem to be asking of doctors inhumanly high standards of skill, intelligence, imagination, patience, and honor. This is unfair, but it is only because of an illusion that doctors themselves have fostered as much as anybody: the illusion of modest infallibility. I noticed as a student, first at my own English university and then at two others in the United States, that medical students were notable for high spirits, coarse humor, and general affability, but not particularly for intellectual brilliance. This cruel reputation must have been planted long ago because practitioners of medicine were regarded for hundreds of years as journeymen, on a level with butchers, carpenters, and barbers, and were denied the term "doctor" for two centuries after it had been bestowed on theologians and lawyers.

But sometime during the nineteenth century—perhaps after surgery turned from amputation to repair—a medical degree descended like a small halo; and ever since, the ordinary citizen has secretly resented it or been dazzled by it. The retention of the serpent as a logo has certainly helped to keep alive the notion of the doctor as the possessor of a strange and subtle wisdom. Cherish and protect this illusion. It has not yet occurred to the layman that doctors—like cab drivers, schoolmasters, politicians, and television repairmen—can be very good, good, indifferent, bad, or downright stupid. Do not let the word get out!

In the meantime, let the conscientious doctor, harried by an excess of sick patients and by his usual large allotment of hypochondriacs, make the most of the peculiar boon offered today by the increasingly numerous varieties of antibiotics and steroids: when you are baffled by the patient's primary affliction, give him another disease and cure that.

A Noble Plan to Dissolve the Union

GIVEN BEFORE THE PHILADELPHIA BAR ASSOCIATION, IN
PHILADELPHIA, TUESDAY, MARCH 9, 1982

A Noble Plan to Dissolve
the Union

You are lucky, as luncheon guests, in knowing that *I* know you must very soon return to the office, the courtroom, the hurt plaintiff, or the innocent defendant. This means that we have a common understanding to cut all preliminary cackle and get down to what has been variously known as the nub, the basics, the nitty-gritty, and the bottom line. Very well, then.

Two things trouble me just now. They concern all of us, and they specially concern lawyers, in a nation in which lawyers loom larger in government than in any other self-governing nation I can think of. It is always a surprise, even to jurists in other countries, to hear that of the fifty-five men who wrote the Constitution more than thirty were lawyers. And it is always a shock to any citizen having a first serious brush with the law to discover what a slow-motion interpretation can be given to the phrase "a speedy and public trial," how long and weary and expensive a journey it can be from the accusation to the verdict, how longer still from the verdict to the final appeal, from the wound to the corrective surgery. As one who has filled his quota of American trials, in several states of the Union, I have had more reasons than most to pass on to newly sworn citizens the sad, cautionary sentence of Judge Learned Hand: "I know no one who has a greater respect, or even reverence, than I for the majesty of the law, but my advice to any American is to spend a lifetime, if possible, avoiding litigation."

The two things that trouble me are, I believe, threats to the federal system of government. Which, if not quite as threatening as Richard Nixon's creation of an autonomous Politburo inside the White House, could get to be as serious as Franklin Roosevelt's attempt to pack the Supreme Court of the United States.

They are, first, the coming attempt to use the Eleventh Amendment, maybe also the Ninth,* to limit the guarantee, in the third article of the Constitution, that "the judicial power shall extend to *all* cases, in law and equity, arising under the Constitution." My second concern is over the move on the part of this administration (a move which in political practice is not far removed from the first) to return to the states certain federal powers and obligations, and to do this in the strangely misnamed cause of "the New Federalism."

On the first issue, the prime move, as we all know, is to see that certain national issues are declared by Congress to be outside the jurisdiction of the United States Supreme Court. This is to be done through the interminable process of a constitutional amendment: a process which, during the long battle toward ratification or rejection, could paralyze, or at least call in question, the overriding authority of the Court on other issues. The ordinary citizen, and any ambitious politician with other dogmatic grievances, might well ask: after busing and abortion and the wishful absurdity of a balanced budget, what next? It

---

*The Eleventh Amendment: "The judicial power of the United States shall not be construed to extend to any suit in law or equity, commenced or prosecuted against one of the United States by citizens of another State, or by citizens of any foreign state."

The Ninth Amendment: "The enumeration in the Constitution of certain rights shall not be construed to deny or disparage others retained by the people."

would not be long, it seems to me, before the state courts would in many matters be encouraged to make claims of authority that would take an even longer time to challenge and defeat.

Tocqueville noticed that "in all the civilized countries of Europe, the government has always shown the greatest repugnance to allow the cases to which it was itself a party to be decided by the courts of justice. This repugnance naturally attains its utmost height in an absolute government." But, he remarked, by way of admirable contrast, "in America the Supreme Court is the sole tribunal of the nation," and he thought that "the power vested [in it] of pronouncing a statute to be unconstitutional forms one of the most powerful barriers which has ever been devised against the tyranny of political assemblies." Fifty years before Tocqueville, Alexander Hamilton was pleading, in the *Federalist* papers, for a single supreme tribunal and arguing against the people who wanted independent states' courts. He wrote: "Thirteen"—there then being thirteen states—"independent courts of final jurisidiction over the same causes, arising from the same laws, is a hydra in government, from which nothing but contradiction and confusion can proceed." And, with his usual gift for telling analogies, he cited from the case of fifteenth-century Germany the exact sort of contradiction and confusion he had in mind: "The power of determining causes between two states, between one state and the citizens of another, and between the citizens of different states, is . . . essential to the peace of the union. . . . History gives us a horrid picture of the dissensions and private wars which distracted and desolated Germany, prior to the institution of the Imperial Chamber by Maximilian . . . . a court invested with authority to decide finally all differences among the members of the Germanic body."

Tocqueville also concluded that the Court was likely to be the best judge of the weight of public opinion, or what Holmes called "the moral climate of the time." May I add the suggestion that the Court, having sat above many battles and watched them, is a safer judge of what had better be done in the interest of public order. As Holmes wrote, in the very first sentence of *The Common Law* (a work we might be celebrating today, for it is just one hundred years old): "The life of the law has not been logic; it has been experience." If this dangerous proposal comes before the House Judiciary Committee, let us hope that Tocqueville, Hamilton, and Holmes will be called to testify.

NOW, for the oxymoron of "the New Federalism." (Oxymoron: from the Greek *oxys* = sharp, and *moros* = foolish: meaning "pointedly contradictory or foolish.")

The theory is a noble one: that the people who live together in different climates, under different conditions, with different means of livelihood, are best able to know and meet their own needs. But once you decentralize a federal bureau and allow a local authority—sometimes only one man—to set the proper standard, you are at the mercy of fifty different standards, dictated no doubt in many places by honest and expert opinion, but just as often by local greed and self-interest. I remember a time, before the Pure Food and Drug Act was strengthened by the Wheeler-Lea Act of 1938, and before the national public health service had much central authority, when the supervision of the public health was so widely, and so wildly, administered that Wisconsin applied possibly the most exacting high standards in the Western world, while the public health commissioner of one western state we shall not mention was a failed pharmacist with a lively interest in the running of the local brothels.

My own view of this new noble experiment—the idea of giving more authority back to the states—is that it is a parallel response to a general movement in the United States to unmelt the melting pot, to break down the goulash of the pot into its ethnic ingredients: to return, in short, to the immigrant compounds which Teddy Roosevelt was determined to fuse into one nation, when he said: "The country must stop talking about German-Americans and Italian-Americans and Polish-Americans. We have room for but one language here, and that is the English language, for we intend to see that the crucible turns our people out as Americans. There must be no more hyphenated Americans."

It is my view that the New Federalism is Old States Rights writ large, and that returning to the states the power—even on the whopping assumption that you can return the money also—the power to take care of the poor and the sick and the old could help along a regression to the condition of the first independent American government, to the Articles of Confederation which, over a dreadful seven years, brought the Union close to bankruptcy and hopeless disunion.

Let me remind you of the condition of this country, of this new republic, two hundred years ago today.*

> Once the war and the celebrations were over, the indissoluble union began to dissolve. Like the victims of a hurricane or a blitz, the old colonists had learned that there is no livelier stimulus to brotherhood than physical danger. But once the storm had passed, they headed for home and went their own ways. They were drunk in the pride of sovereignty, but not as Americans: as New Yorkers, Georgians, Marylanders, Vermonters—and so much so that they began to act like independent nations. The states hemmed in by other states were frantic to stake claims to the unsettled lands in the West. They developed their own money systems and levied their own taxes and ignored their neighbors. Some of them began to start their own relations with foreign countries . . . . Everybody wanted to raise his own crops, make his own products, without a thought of the national market. In some states they regressed to barter.

*From the author's *America.*

They improvised their own boycott of each other's goods, slapped tariffs on arriving cargoes, and shucked off the huge national debt as somebody else's business.

That failed experiment was due to the failure to give any overriding power to a *national* legislature. It was little written or talked about when, six years ago, we pretended to celebrate the birth of American independence. What we were celebrating was the outbreak of a war. Two hundred years ago today, the Republic was floundering in an orgy of states' rights under the misnomer of a confederation. 1987 will be the great year to commemorate, for it will mark the two hundredth anniversary of the time when the influential men in their own states came to this city, flouted their instructions to revamp the Articles of Confederation, dumped them, honestly agreed that the first form of republican government had been a disastrous experiment, and sat down to try again, to write a constitution, to set practical limits to the powers of the states, and to invent a national federation of the state governments.

I don't doubt that the legislators and lobbyists of Washington, D.C., today can and do harbor corruption; but not as much, I think, as the legislators and lobbyists of fifty separate states acting out of sight of a federal policeman.

The motto on the seal of the United States was taken by Franklin and Jefferson and John Adams from Virgil. It does not say "Out of One, Many." It says *E Pluribus Unum,* "Out of Many, One."

Of course, we are always hearing that we are a plural society. But if we are not to fragment, on great public issues, into a collection of quarreling German republics, with incipient Quebecs in our future, we had better think twice about weakening the independence of any one of the three branches of government; about denying any litigant—whether a state, a city, a corporation, a President, or any ordinary citizen—the ultimate guarantee that we are "one": which means, in the first matter, the guarantee of a truly Supreme Court; and, in the second matter, the promise—which the lives of Lloyd George and Franklin Roosevelt, the rise of Communist states, the proliferation of self-governing republics on all continents in this century have made compulsory—the promise that national governments shall exercise a national responsibility for the protection of the poor, the sick, the young, the disabled, and the dispossessed. It is time to stress the *Unum* in *E Pluribus Unum*.

What to Preserve, and Why

GIVEN BEFORE THE NATIONAL TRUST FOR HISTORIC
PRESERVATION, AT PALM BEACH, FLORIDA,
JANUARY 9, 1983

What to Preserve, and Why

Since this lecture inaugurates a series, to be given by architectural experts around the country, it would be reasonable to hope that it might strike an uplifting, at least an inspirational, note. But I am not an uplifter or an inspirer. By profession, I am a reporter. By choice, this time, I am also a nagger.

Many years ago, the late Prime Minister Clement Attlee, who was that blessed rarity, a monosyllabic politician, was approached by a colleague who suggested that at the first session of the new Parliament he might adopt the American tradition whereby the head of government makes a long oratorical speech entitled "The State of the Nation." Attlee replied: "Certainly not! I shall say what's on my mind." I shall say what's on my mind.

Because we are meeting on the Sabbath, I am moved, like the gentlemen of the cloth, to begin with a text. I take my text, then, from the Reverend—or the Very Irreverend—Tom Wolfe: "O Beautiful, for spacious skies, for amber waves of grain, has there ever been another place on earth where so many people of wealth and power have paid for, and put up with, so much architecture they detested as within thy blessed borders today?"

This is not a rhetorical question. Not in the mouth of Tom Wolfe. The answer is, no, never, anywhere. It is, however, a serious and fascinating question. It goes beyond Mr. Wolfe's lament over the craven dependence, of so many powerful Americans, on the architectural styles of Europe—first at their most grandiose, and then at their most monumentally bleak. It goes, first, to the question of why an American, once he left his lean-to cabin or his clapboard cottage, or even his honest and graceful little Colonial house, and made a million, why he should yearn, like Mr. Frick, to house himself in a French *pavillon,* or, like the grandson of a ferryboat captain, Mr. Vanderbilt, in a massive Renaissance palace. Or why the lowly saloonkeepers of San Francisco who sank a lucky pick in the Comstock Lode should fetch over Italian marble and French furniture in shiploads for their mansions on Nob Hill. Forgive this rather snobbish stress on their origins. It is only to make the point that it was new money which felt it must go one better than, say, the comfortable little townhouse that Emerson lived in, or the New York brownstone of the Roosevelts. One of those Nobs, James C. Flood, who once brewed fish stew for hungry businessmen, may have seemed to resist the European mania by importing, for his mansion, Connecticut brownstone. But he did this under a misapprehension he picked up on a visit to New York: that it was the façade of choice among the rich. By the time he was told that on the contrary it was the preference of old, stuffy, and merely comfortable families, it was too late—he was stuck with it. But he could console himself with the thought that, like a New Yorker importing some baroque object from three thousand miles away, he too had imported an exotic from three thousand miles away. It was, anyway, unique in San Francisco. As, I believe, it still is—in scale, at any rate, rising there today as the very solid, the very somber, the very glum home of the Pacific Union Club on Nob Hill.

This lament, for the view of Europe as a huge antique shop there for the looting by rich Americans, is of course a very old and monotonous theme. We won't dwell on it, except to remind ourselves (what British and French visitors, especially, either don't know or have forgotten) that at some time even old money was new money, and that the impulse to advertise one's prosperity with foreign doodads or native imitations ran through English society in the eighteenth and early nineteenth centuries, at the latest, and by then it was an impulse indulged by both merchants and kings. Of course, English kings, being only in our own time of preponderantly English blood, had always looked on Europe as their hometown display center of the materials and styles they would use for the building and decoration of their palaces. They had brought over Dutchmen to paint the royal portraits, and Italians to paint the royal frescoes. Later ones stacked Buckingham Palace with nothing but French furniture. You could go so far as to say that if Inigo Jones had not gone to Italy and fallen in love with Palladio, we should have been denied all the Palladian treasures, large and small, of English architecture; and if it had not been for that new fashion in monumental, but drafty and uncomfortable, houses, Alexander Pope would have spared us his mockery of such buildings that

> Call the winds thro' long arcades to roar
> Proud to catch cold at a Venetian door.

It was during, and just beyond, the Regency that the itch to appear more equal, and quainter, than one's neighbors could be scratched by both King and commoner. The Prince Regent, celebrating the fact that Britain had become the paramount interloper in India, called on John Nash to transform the Royal Pavilion at Brighton in "the Hindoo style." The new merchant class built itself little Italian villas, with French windows no less, in the latest smart suburb. Were it not for Thomas Hope, who was originally excluded from the Royal Academy for what were thought to be his ridiculous furniture designs (chests in the shape of Grecian urns, tabletops supported by caryatids or Greek maidens with snakes in their hair), there might have been no Regency style. And if James Gibbs had not added his daring signature, of a steeple on top of a classical portico, to the church of St. Martin in the Fields, we might not have had the characteristic facade of the New England Colonial church. Even into our own century, the British landscape has been peppered with bungalows, originally a style imported by retired civil servants and army officers who wanted to show they were home from India, if not from Bengal (whence "bungalow" takes its name).

So, next time some snooty visitor from overseas drops a patronizing remark about a French villa in Newport or an Austrian-type ski lodge in Colorado, you might retort with the line that the outrageous Calvin Trillin attributed to Alexander Haig on meeting the King of the Belgians: "Well, I'm a Hapsburg on my mother's side, so lah-de-dah!"

The main complaint of Tom Wolfe is not, however, about the imitative taste of the Robber Barons and their successors, new to grandeur and therefore seizing "safe" styles to boost their social insecurity. It is about the mass prostration, before one *modern* European style, of Americans who no longer need to defer to Europe in power, in distinction, or in their knowledge of a long-native American tradition. In other words, he's talking about the willing enslavement of American corporations, and the architects they employ, to Gropius, Mies van der Rohe, the whole Bauhaus school, and the so-called International Style. (We ought to recall that this style was conceived by very earnest men, who were also upper-middle-class aesthetes, as a proper style for workers' apartment houses and one that would liberate them from the poky, ugly stuffiness of their own small separate castles. Nobody that I've heard of ever asked the honest workingman if he welcomed this clinical escape hatch. It was what the Internationalists thought he ought to have. Whether he wanted it or not, within a couple of generations his superiors had succeeded in depositing him in the prison of a high-rise housing development.)

What was not anticipated in the dawn glow of this act of noblesse oblige, and what is the burden of Tom Wolfe's lament, and mine, is the baffling fact that this workers' apartment house, enlarged into a giant, was imported as the only model with which to transform and denude the native American invention of the skyscraper. Nobody has explained satisfactorily how and why, forty years later, American architects, or the German masters themselves, were—at the behest of board chairmen—cluttering the skyscapes of New York, Pittsburgh, Dallas, Houston, Los Angeles, and, alas, the unique American city of San Francisco with enormously expensive, mammoth monoliths of steel and plate glass and concrete, with mysterious white cylinders and metal staircases and prison corridors. Tom Wolfe tells about a couple he knew who put up a $900,000 summerhouse, obediently built to the prescribed design, and "were driven to the edge of sensory deprivation by the whiteness and the lightness and leanness and cleanness and bareness and spareness of it all. They became desperate for an antidote, such as coziness and color. They tried to bury the obligatory white sofas under Thai-silk throw pillows of every rebellious, iridescent shade of magenta, pink, and tropical green imaginable. But the architect returned, as he always does, like the conscience of a Calvinist, and he lectured them and hectored them and chucked the shimmering little sweet things out."

Well, you'll be relieved to hear that this passionate primal scream introduces my theme. Which is: what to preserve, and why. (If this talk had been requested by a government department, I suppose I should have had to call it "Prioritization, and the Implementation of Alternate Options, in the Concept of Preservation.")

I'm sure that one of the besetting problems of your board

of advisers is the annoying fact that people want to preserve what *they* like, what *they* approve of. You may have gathered that if I had my way, if I could be benevolent dictator of the United States for a year, I should provide several million jobs for the wrecking industry. The glorious swinging ball would thunder through the land as it demolished row after towering row of concrete honeycombs, steel-and-glass curtains, the titanic glass boxes designed to give cataracts to people working under fluorescent light, the factory that is not a factory but an insurance temple or a hotel, which yet hopes to fool the people by calling itself something like the Chesterfield or the Belvedere or the Taj Mahal. Then there would be a million more jobs for the construction industry. Never mind where the money would come from. It would come from Congress sure enough, provided its members first took an oath that they deplored big deficits and were devoted to a balanced budget.

Plainly, sadly, this will not do. I am obviously a bigot. And my bigotry derives from a phrase, a criterion of worth, that was fed to me at a tender age. I think it was Clive Bell who first coined what he took to be a final definition of a work of art, whether it was a painting, a building, a poem, or a chair. He said that the best works of art are finished products that preserve "a valuable state of mind." A valuable state of mind. That's what we tense college boys dashed around looking for, although it got to be difficult for a young man to keep his eye on the object. There were times when such a finished product as a beautifully designed young woman looked more like a valuable state of mind than, say, a commode.

But, like all original definitions, however scoffed at later, this one was a serviceable phrase, especially for people who would later be called preservationists. My distinguished college supervisor was very fond of this foot rule, and never more so than when the wrecking ball took its toll of the last section of Nash's Regent Street. The demolition of that marvelous street (which none of us has ever seen except in Mr. Ackermann's lithographs) was—said E. M. W. Tillyard—the obliteration of a valuable state of mind, an act of public immorality. I think his anger was well taken. I share it whenever visitors to these shores ask me where they can see, in sequence, the early, the middle, the late work of Frank Lloyd Wright. Some examples of each period can be ferreted out by the patient detective, and odd houses here and there are jealously advertised. But much of the best has gone with the wind and the developers. Similarly, New York City started disastrously late to protect much of its best and most characteristic architecture. By the time we woke up to the somber grace and the originality of Aldrich and White's American Romanesque buildings on Park Avenue south of Fifty-seventh Street, they had succumbed to monolithitis.

Because it is obvious that I still hold to the strictures I was brought up on, you'll gather that I would be an impossible member of your board: a renegade approving only what is Georgian, either in its native land or in its Colonial and Federal (and, I must add, its tropical) derivations; registering a nay vote against everything that betrays the blessing of the very heavy hand of Queen Victoria or of the architects and furnishers of her middle and late years. I must exempt from this taboo, however, the rearguard resistance of Ashbee in his Chelsea houses, the brave simplifications of Voysey in many places; and, in America, the midcentury Frenchified houses of some Southern towns, as well as, of course, the simpler Greek Revival mansions, some Italianate brownstones in New York, and, at the end of the century, the Gingerbread Boys, who had such fun making houses out of lace patterns.

I am not, from your point of view, beyond salvation. Or, should I say, beyond second thoughts? Years ago, my own dogmatic tastes, which I assumed were those of my generation and the one before that, were given a jolt by the discovery that one of the classic New England churches, the lovely Congregational church at Litchfield, Connecticut, was thought so offensive to the "decent" taste of the 1870s that it was replaced by a Victorian Gothic horror, and the original was carted out of town to become, in turn, a dance hall, an armory, and a movie house. Not until the encrusted Victorian scales had fallen from the eyes of the citizens forty or more years later was this masterpiece carted back into town and replanted on its original site.

An even more startling (to me) example of a revolution in public taste was demonstrated in 1834, when the Houses of Parliament were destroyed by fire. Smartly on hand were two architects who, very much in tune with the advanced taste of their day, loathed Georgian and Regency architecture and saw in the consuming flames the wrath of God. (There is, I find, no truth in the suggestion that they set the bonfire.) One of them, a Frenchman's son and a Catholic convert, Augustus Pugin, put out a hectoring pamphlet attacking what he called "the meanness and vulgarity," and nauseating worldliness, of Nash and the whole domesticated classical style. The time was at hand, he announced, for a revival of the Gothic or "true Christian" architecture. And so, God save us, it was.

But my real reformation—my late discovery that my idea of a valuable state of mind might not be the right criterion for a preservation society—came one evening some years ago when I was invited to attend a small dinner to honor an English architect, president of a preservation society, who happened also to be of the blood royal. Naturally, even dedicated enemies among our leading architects rushed to break bread with him. After dinner, we played a game. We were issued slips of paper and told to write down our choice of the two ugliest buildings in New York City. I looked furtively round the table. There were at least two men there, of deafening fame, who were practicing American disciples of the Great White Gods, of Gropius and Mies van der Rohe. Out of an elementary instinct for self-protection, if not from simple good manners, I crossed their bleak constructions from my mind. At the end, we were asked in turn to declare ourselves. I was confident that the group would applaud my insight and my choices. My number two was the Armory at Ninety-fourth Street and Madison Avenue. But the certain number one—an incomparable Victorian monster of pomposity and muddleheadedness, with its elephantine mass, its grimy brick and stony trim, its warehouse clutter of ledges, turrets, towers, gables, chimneys, its mean, heavy-lidded windows peeking out on Central Park like hooded owls with the flu—was Hardenburgh's Horror: the Dakota Apartment House at Seventy-second Street and Central Park West.

I expected instant, warm applause. But well-bred shock and consternation fell on the group. I discovered (a little late in the evening, I must say) that all those present were founding members of the American branch of the English society over which His Grace presided: the *Victorian* Preservation Society! The Armory and the Dakota were, no doubt, down on their list as jewels to be protected and marveled at by future generations, preferably with federal funds. One of the disciples of St. Gropius turned to me and said: "I suppose you think that domestic architecture came to a stop about 1860?" "Right," I said, "or even earlier, any day after Thomas Cubitt finished Belgravia and Eaton Square."

It was after that disastrous occasion that I communed with myself and began to see that perhaps the job of the preservationist was not to preserve only what was lovely and of good report. That might be all right for you and me, in our own street, our own neighborhood. But if you are to preserve on a national scale, it is going to be impossible to agree on what, in any given place, is "valuable" to most people. Some people would maintain that you could learn a lot about the vanished life and times of Chicago, or Baton Rouge, or Sacramento by preserving relics of the state of mind of the people who lived there—whether valuable or not. What Clive Bell really meant by "valuable," I had to admit, was what was admirable to him.

And, let us say, the red brick rows of Baltimore houses, with their little scrubbed white steps, may not be the prettiest streets in America, but they tell us something about the ideas of neatness and family pride that a generation or two of poor people believed in. The original hospital building of Johns Hopkins is just the sort of Victorian nightmare that makes me think of a hospital as the Last Stop before Purgatory. But its design may be worth recalling, if only as a reminder that the top floor was reserved for respiratory cases: it was farthest from the fields, and therefore from the mists that wafted disease along the ground. A visible monument to the miasmic theory of disease, before the discovery of microorganisms.

You see that I am approaching, albeit in a labored way, your own superior definition of the aim of preservation: "public participation in the preservation of sites, buildings and objects *significant* in American history and culture." By the way, I believe it was Clive Bell also who coined the phrase "significant form."

Once you establish this test and start working on it, you also discover, and surely you have discovered, how desperately late in the day it is to try now and preserve some of the most significant sites, buildings, and objects of even nineteenth-century American culture. I think of several sad examples from my own experience when, a dozen years ago, I was traveling thousands of miles around this country doing the reconnaissance work for my television history of America.

To talk about the Mormon experiment in Utah, I wanted to give it a true visual character at the start by filming the road south from Spanish Fork down to the temple at Manti, which is bordered by what became known in the West as the Mormon tree: the Lombardy poplar. My director went off alone to look it over. He telephoned me from somewhere along the once-beautiful Route 89. He said, "There isn't a poplar in sight." He was right.

When I was about to film a program called "Domesticating a Wilderness," I thought of two tiny towns on the Kansas prairie, only two miles apart, which together wove two vital strands in the character and life, and prosperity, of the state. One was Victoria, a minute town founded and named by Sir George Grant and a dozen or so leisurely English remittance men whose mental vision of the West—the hunting of wild beasts and wild women, and playing endless faro on steamboats—fell short of the reality by about twelve hundred miles. They got bored and were not so much run out of town as eclipsed by the industrious settlers two miles to the north, in Catherine, so called because it was founded, in the 1870s, by Russians (or rather by the descendants of Germans whom Catherine the Great had brought into Russia to improve the farming). These diligent people built a town in the shape of a circular palisade, with no doors and windows on the outside. They had heard about the Indians. I had seen this strange, this unique, town as late as 1934. My director called me from there. He told me I was hallucinating. "It looks," he said, "like a little Montclair." We had to make the main points by photographing the name of Grant, painted and peeling on the high school baseball stand: Grant introduced to this country Black Angus cattle. Two miles away, it was enough (it *had* to be enough) for me to stand in an ocean of wheat and simply say that these old "Roosians" introduced Turkey Red Wheat, and so made possible the feeding of the Allied armies in the First World War.

You might have thought that when we came to do the universal mad rush for gold, we'd have been spoiled for choice of ghost towns. I showed my director on a map a dozen or so I'd known, in Nevada, Arizona, California. He was gone for a couple of weeks. He reported that there was only one left, 8000 feet up in the Sierras. It was, it is, Bodie—once teeming with life and silver and vice, now windblown and deserted. But it was there for us. The state of California has kept it—not decorated it or restored it, or decked out the neighboring citizens with Victorian skirts and mining picks and pans. It is there as it was when the veins gave out.

So, while regretting that you didn't go into business until 1949, I have to congratulate you on how far you've come. You began, as I understand it, by preserving the old town of Charleston, South Carolina. (I wish you'd gone to work at once and persuaded them to bury or tear down their telephone poles and the network of wires that made it impossible for us to film the best stretch of houses. We had to decamp and film Savannah instead.) But now, I read, you have gone beyond the preservation of threatened houses, parks, historic monuments, and the like and are renovating slums, old factories, turning run-down wharves into recreation plazas, and even attempting to implant an artificial heart into the bodies of soulless developers. I am impressed to think that this imaginative view of renewal not only melts a frozen image of a vanished America, but attacks in a direct and humane way the rotting streets and districts where poverty lives and crime battens on it.

I will end with a suggestion, which may be naive or impertinent, since you may well have been laboring at it for years. But just in case it's not so. It is the idea not so much of preservation as of renewal, not by building up but by tearing down. Not houses. Not office buildings. I have in mind two characteristic blots on our landscape, from coast to coast, which we've all come to take for granted.

About twenty-five years ago, a distinguished American newspaper published a series of articles projecting the semi-industrial takeover of the West Country of England. Doomsday was fixed at something like 1970. I persuaded a friend and his wife to embark with us on a farewell tour of Hampshire, Wiltshire, Dorset, Somerset, Devon, and Cornwall.

We had not been on the road for more than a day or two when my friend remarked, "My God, it's like a private park." I suppressed the pedagogic impulse to inquire, "And what, pray, makes a stretch of landscape look like a private park?" He never did guess the answer to this unspoken question. No wonder: it is difficult to see what's not there. So, while this vast parkland was there to enjoy, I mentioned that my entry for the most civilized bill passed by a Parliament since the Second World War was the Town and Country Planning Act of 1951, whereby billboards were banned in the open countryside of Britain everywhere beyond a distance of two miles from a town center.

The second clue to my friend's amazement was also unspotted, being also invisible. No telegraph poles. In open country, that is. These two simple and, I admit, very drastic prohibitions have done wonders in restoring the landscape not, perhaps, to its pristine state (which would no doubt have looked uncouth to the English after the seventeenth century) but to that tamed, and marvelously tailored, landscape that is rural England. These two taboos do not detract, either, from the more majestic parts of the island; they are silent reminders that, for the time being, the Yahoo has been checked.

I surely ought not to leave this topic, this wishful and hopeless vision of America with buried wires and no hint of outdoor advertising, without sending up a cheer for Vermont, the only state in the Union, I believe, which banishes all billboards from its landscape.

There is a final note I hate to sound. But it is constantly struck by practical and anxious men and women in our country and in all the countries of Europe. It is the note of misgiving, or of scorn, from people who look on preservation as a brave or frivolous little rearguard action against the inevitability of nuclear annihilation. Certainly the men and women we elect to government ignore or neglect this apocalyptic question at the peril of their duty, not to mention their souls. But we on the outside, once we have aired our opinion, and voted, and taken our stand, must go on living our lives "as if" this country, this civilization, will endure.

Thirty years ago, I had to address this question in the preface to a collection of radio talks which covered a gamut of American themes from the most deadly serious to the lively hilarious. I make no apology for saying it over again, to you now. For even though to some people it may sound like a whistling solo in a graveyard, I believe it still to be true. This is it:

> Even the prospect of early annihilation should not keep us from making the most of our days on this unhappy planet. In the best of times, our days are numbered, anyway. And it would be a crime against Nature for any generation to take the world crisis so solemnly that it put off doing and enjoying those things for which we were presumably designed in the first place, and which the gravest statesmen and the hoarsest politicians hope to make available to all men in the end: I mean the opportunity to do good work, to fall in love, to enjoy friends, to sit under trees, to read, to hit a ball, to bounce the baby.

Now, may I thank you for your sportsmanship in coming indoors, and for your patience in *staying* here on a beautiful Sunday afternoon. May I also thank you for the felicitous choice of this date, since it is the eve of my wife's birthday—and I am not alone in thinking of her as, among other things, a splendid example of historic preservation. Thank you.

The American in England:
Emerson to S. J. Perelman

THE REDE LECTURE, GIVEN AT THE SENATE HOUSE,
CAMBRIDGE, ENGLAND, MAY 8, 1975

The Rede Lecture is probably the oldest public lecture in continuous existence. Sir Robert Rede, who became Chief Justice of the Common Pleas in 1506, founded three public lectureships in Cambridge. In 1858, the endowment was reorganized to provide for one annual lecture, "to be delivered by a man of eminence in science or literature." In modern times, the lecturers have included Max Beerbohm, André Maurois, P. M. S. Blackett, Kenneth Clark, Herbert Butterfield, and C. P. Snow, whose lecture *The Two Cultures and The Scientific Revolution* became a topic of national controversy.

The American in England:
Emerson to S. J. Perelman

When any public man—that is to say, a man who has become a successful exhibitionist in any field—is invited to do a lecture under auspices as majestic as these, there is a danger that he will succumb to what I must call the Sullivan–Conan Doyle syndrome.

Sir Arthur Sullivan left W. S. Gilbert and broke up the long Savoy partnership because, we are told, he found their personal relationship no longer tolerable. But the relationship became increasingly irksome because of a root cause in Sullivan himself: which was his conviction that the Savoy operas were frivolous stuff unworthy of an eminent Victorian, and that it was time to reassert his genius as a serious composer. So, having proved himself incomparable as a musical mimic of Handel and Mozart and Rossini and Gounod and Mendelssohn and Verdi; having scored for a small orchestra more exquisitely than anyone before him; and having produced—in *Iolanthe*—the most delicious comic opera in the language, he reverted to his earliest ambition: which was to write sacred music of deafening mediocrity.

Conan Doyle was a victim of the same menopausal delusion of grandeur. He had conceived the most memorable single character in English fiction. He had developed from mixed origins the pure detective thriller, a form that gives no sign of ever dying off. But he grew to be ashamed of this one unique talent and was moved to write "literature." And so he devoted himself to martial epics that are unread today, and will be unread tomorrow or the day after, for the stark reason that they are works of stupefying dullness.

In a smaller, but no less threatening, way a mere broadcaster is similarly tempted to desert his normal trade, which in these surroundings he is apt to think fit only for lie-a-bed plumbers, housewives, politicians, and other secular Sunday-morning laggards, and turn to a theme worthy of an ancient university and the magnificoes I see all around me. The almost irresistible temptation is to rise to the occasion. Ladies and gentlemen, I shall try not to rise to the occasion.

I am tempted to begin with one of the first American expatriates, who achieved the ultimate ambition of all succeeding Anglophiles by hobnobbing with the King himself. He was a member of the first graduating class of Harvard. He came to England in the useful disguise of a divine, and by first betraying his royalist friends to Cromwell, and then his Cromwellian friends to Charles the Second, his services to the Crown—which were almost exclusively exercised in intrigue, espionage, and murder—were rewarded with a knighthood and a lavish sum of money. Out of which it was possible later on to found, and to give his name to, a Cambridge college. It occurs to me, perhaps a little late in the day, that this is not the time or place to bring him up. So we will not even mention the name—of Sir George Downing.

I want to talk about the way certain representative Americans felt about England and the English at first hand—and vice versa—from the time Americans began to think of themselves as foreigners down to our own time. The English tend not to know about this, about the large and prickly body of American comments on England, even when they are well acquainted with the long and impressive record of British comments on America—which begins with the gaudy publicity handouts of Hakluyt, Michael Drayton, and Ben Jonson, none of whom had ever been to America or was destined to.

The British literature on America remains generally inquisitive and fair-minded until the War of Independence, since until then it was assumed that Americans were expatriate Englishmen doing interesting, if peculiar, things in a strange landscape. But the defeat in the War of Independence inflicted a trauma on the English. George the Third, it was said, could not bear to look on the engraving of Lord Cornwallis's surrender at Yorktown. He found it inconceivable that his crack troops had been beaten by what he called "a rabble" of guerrillas, and he drew up an instrument of abdication, which—as we all know—was politely ignored. But from then on, by way of punishment, American history vanished from the English schoolbooks, the American became a heretic and a foreigner, and the comments of English travelers about him became as waspish as that remark of a British admiral on hearing, in 1947, that India had won her independence: "They'll jolly soon find out it'll never be the same."

So—by the turn of the eighteenth century (certainly after the war of 1812, in which the Americans had the gall to prove they could whip the British by sea if not by land) it became almost impossible for an Englishman to write dispassionately about America; and for an American visiting England to appear without chips on his shoulders the size of epaulettes.

From the beginning, then, of America as an independent nation, we have both been the victims of a complementary neurosis: of a defensive paranoia, under the influence of which the American is determined to prove that the English, though elegant, are effete; and the Englishman is not going to be impressed by the prodigal who cockily left home, and stayed, and—what's worse—grew rich.

I have been careful to talk of England and not of Britain, because to Americans Ireland, on account of its normal social ease and urge to be liked, is not a foreign country at all; Scotland is as separate a nation as many of its sons and daughters wish it were; and to an American Wales is as alien as Tibet.

I suppose that Anglo-American relations, so called, have never been so childishly irritable as they were in the twenty years or so after the war of 1812. The official English tone was set by the most influential of British journals in a scornful piece which began: *"Who sees an American play? Who reads an American book?"* The Americans themselves, it has to be said, were as much to blame for this derision as anybody. For while thousands of pioneers were pushing into the lands beyond the Appalachians and singing about their new life, they hadn't much time to write about it. The arbiters of American letters remained in Boston, Philadelphia, and the Southern seaboard and were still overcome by the urge to compete with the English in gentility and the field of beautiful letters. Which brought them, and brings us, to the thunderbolt of Ralph Waldo Emerson's Phi Beta Kappa address to Harvard in 1837, which he called "The American Scholar."

It starts out almost as a whimsical, overspun essay on the uses of books. Until he propounds the unscholarly idea that books simply provide a vocabulary for life in action. "Beware," he says, "of receiving truth from another mind, though it were in torrents of light. Genius is always sufficiently the enemy of genius by over-influence. . . . the English dramatic poets have Shakespearized now for two hundred years." So—"meek young men grow up in libraries, believing it their duty to accept the views which Cicero, which Locke, which Bacon, have given; forgetful that Cicero, Locke, and Bacon were only young men in libraries who wrote these books. Hence, instead of Man Thinking, we have the bookworm. Hence the book-learned class, who value books, as such. . . . Hence the restorers of readings, the emendators, the bibliomaniacs of all degrees." Then "what is the right use of books? . . . they are for nothing but to inspire. I had better never see a book than to be warped by its attraction clean out of my own orbit, and made a satellite instead of a system."

These words made the listening dons uncomfortable enough to see that Emerson was banished from talking at Harvard again for another twenty-eight years. But there were also students there—of law and medicine and literature—who got the point sufficiently to form a company, a dozen years later, and head for Missouri and the two-thousand-mile walk to California and the gold fields.

It was at the end of his lecture that Emerson struck the note which provoked Oliver Wendell Holmes to call his whole address "Our Intellectual Declaration of Independence."

"I ask not for the great, the remote, the romantic; what is doing in Italy or Arabia; what is Greek art, or Provençal minstrelsy. . . . Give me insight into today, and you may have the antique and future worlds. What would we really know the meaning of? The meal in the firkin . . . the ballad in the street . . . the news of the boat . . . the glance of the eye . . . the shop, the plough and ledger. . . . We have listened too long to the courtly muses of Europe. The spirit of the American freeman is already suspected to be timid, imitative, tame. . . . we will walk on our own feet; we will work with our own hands; we will speak our own minds."

Telescoped this way, I must say it sounds a little too quixotic and hairy-chested, a little too like the late Sir Arthur Quiller-Couch's parody of Walt Whitman:

Behold! I am not one that goes to Lectures or the
    pow-wow of Professors.
The elementary laws never apologize: neither do I
    apologize . . .

Myself only I sing. Me Imperturbe. Me Prononcé!
Me progressive and the depth of me progressive.

Yet Emerson was as learned as any of his listeners, but his
knowledge of European literature and science did not obscure
for him the novelty and the pith of the native life around him.
Four years before that famous lecture he had paid his first visit
to England, as an unknown, but he was neither cowed nor def-
erential. He thought of himself, with confident modesty, as the
first of those "American freemen" who were to invade these
shores and make their own observations of the natives without
the hampering afflictions of either Anglophilia or Anglophobia.

Emerson's first surprise was in finding a country with a
benign climate and a countryside "combed and rolled till the
fields appear to have been finished with a pencil instead of a
plough." Here, he says—anticipating generations of later visitors
from New England and the prairie—"here is no winter" (and
no summer either) . . . "no hour in the whole year when one
cannot work." But, "a constant rain—a rain with every tide,"
so that the land is lush and "abounds with game, and at one
season the lakes contain one part water and two parts fish."
There was every resource for industry: "water, stone, potter's
clay, coal, salt and iron. The only drawback on this industrial
conveniency is the darkness of its sky. The night and day are
too nearly of a color. . . . Add the coal smoke. In the manufacturing towns, the fine soot . . . darkens the day, gives white sheep
the color of black sheep, discolors the human saliva, contami-
nates the air, poisons many plants and corrodes the monuments
and buildings." This was true down through my own boyhood
and youth, through the 1950s in fact. Only, in Manchester, we
called the sooty air simply "the weather," and the film of cor-
rosion on the buildings "patina."

As Emerson moved around—and he went from London

to the West Country, to the Midlands and the Scottish high-
lands—he readily absorbed and ignored all the trivial oddities
and differences that are the lifeblood of musical comedies and
skittish movies. He became more and more impressed with a
land of immense wealth and he was shocked by its shameless
ostentation, very much as Englishmen in America were to be
shocked the other way round fifty or sixty years later. Indeed,
you could take the following passage and by substituting
"America" for "England," and "Americans" for "Englishmen,"
you could read it as a regulation English lament on American
civilization:

"There is no country in which so absolute a homage is paid
to wealth. In America there is a touch of shame when a man
exhibits the evidences of large property, as if after all it needed
apology. . . . But . . . a coarse logic rules throughout all English
souls—if you have merit, can you not show it by your good
clothes and coach and horses? . . . In exact proportion is the
reproach of poverty. They do not wish to be represented except
by opulent men."

Yet he was equally impressed by the energy and practicality
of the people: "the best," he called it, "of actual nations," and
yet one which, having "inoculated all nations with her civilization, intelligence and tastes," was now surely at the culmination
of her power, "in its solstice, or already declining." This was
four years before the coronation of Queen Victoria, before the
fruits of the Industrial Revolution had burgeoned in the land
of its birth. He came back fourteen years later, in the dire
depression of 1847, which—far from confirming him in his
gloomy prophecy—made him change his mind, because he noticed (and said it better than anybody) that the English were
even more indomitable in hard times than in prosperity.

He spoke—by now a famous transatlantic figure—before
a banquet in Manchester, which Cobden attended and to which

Dickens sent a letter of apology for his absence. "In this time," he said, "of gloom and commercial disaster, of affliction and beggary in these districts," he thought it best to remind them that he had never expected the British island to be "a lotus-garden." He had learned on the contrary that it was "a cold, foggy, mournful country, where nothing grew well in the open air but robust men and virtuous women . . . that their best parts were slowly revealed; their virtues did not come out until they quarreled; they did not strike twelve the first time . . . and you could know little good of them till you had seen them in action; that in prosperity they were moody and dumpish, but in adversity they were grand. . . . And so, gentlemen, I feel in regard to this aged England, with the possessions, honors and trophies, and also with the infirmities of a thousand years gathering around her, irretrievably committed as she now is to many old customs which cannot suddenly be changed; pressed upon by the transitions of trade and new and incalculable modes, fabrics, arts, machines and competing populations—I see her not dispirited, not weak . . . indeed . . . she sees a little better in a cloudy day, and in storm of battle and calamity she has a secret vigor and a pulse like a cannon. . . . So be it! If it be not so, if the courage of England goes with the chances of a commercial crisis, I will go back to the capes of Massachusetts and my own Indian stream, and say to my countrymen, the old race are gone, and the elasticity and hope of mankind must henceforth remain on the Alleghany ranges, or nowhere."

Well, as you can imagine, that let off in the Free-Trade Hall a bombardment of applause that has not been equaled since, I daresay, by Cobden or John Bright or Lloyd George, or even by the Beatles.

If this has a rather florid Churchillian ring about it, he was —I think—simply a generous man responding with the best of his hopes to the misery he had seen on the streets around him. His curiosity was too probing to blind him to the human price of the throbbing factories and the cyclical penalty of their productiveness. "The robust rural Saxon degenerates in the mills to the Leicester stockinger, to the imbecile Manchester spinner—far on the way to be spiders and needles. The incessant repetition of the same handwork dwarfs the man . . . and presently in a change of industry, whole towns are sacrificed like ant-hills when cotton takes the place of linen, railways of turnpikes. . . . 'Tis not, I suppose, want of probity, so much as the tyranny of trade, which necessitates a perpetual competition of underselling, and that again a perpetual deterioration of the fabric. The machinery has proved, like the balloon, unmanageable, and flies away with the aeronaut."

This was, at the time, a startling and original observation. (Engels had drafted it into an indictment three years before, but his *Condition of the Working Class in England* was not published in English until fifty years later.) And Emerson's remarks, which today would sound like the kettle calling the pan black, came in those days very honestly from an American. For America had not yet struck petroleum, or invented the refinery, the electric bulb, the ore freighter, cheap steel, or the assembly line. There was not yet even a permanent factory population. And around the Great Lakes, where the blast furnaces were to arise and where steel was to be king, they were planting the Catawba wine grape. It was a nation of busy ports, grain markets, and small merchant cities; but in the main a land of yeoman farmers in which Andrew Jackson could boast that there would never be any slums.

I have stayed with Emerson so long because, to me, above all the subsequent commentaries that have come out of America, or for that matter Europe, the book he published ten years after his last visit here—*English Traits*—is incomparable. He is less doctrinaire than Engels. He is as alert to peculiarities of manners and modes as André Maurois. He is wittier than Renier, who wrote the provocative study *The English—Are They Human?* Not as sensitive surely as Henry James to the social subtleties of the upper classes, but more acutely aware of the interplay and collision of *all* classes. And he is more disinterested than any of them.

After him, the tone of most American writing turns political, as the Civil War comes on. And when it came, the Americans who felt most comfortable in England were Southerners or others who shared the strong British partisanship for the Confederate cause: which sprang naturally from a prejudice in favor of a landed aristocracy and realistically from the denial of the cotton that provided the raw material for British manufactures. I have no doubt that the most honorable item of American comment on England at that time is a letter—still proudly on display in Manchester—a letter which Abraham Lincoln wrote to the cotton workers of Lancashire in gratitude for the two years of unemployment and hunger they'd brought on themselves by refusing to unload the cargoes that had managed to run the Union blockade.

After the war, an American arrived who seemed to confirm all the horrors of American journalism that twenty years earlier Dickens had so lovingly deplored. The man came out of darkest Africa with obviously forged letters. He presumed—I think that is the word—to have known the sainted Dr. Livingstone. Henry M. Stanley, the British press decided, was a liar, and probably a Welsh bastard as well. When Livingstone's family authenticated Stanley's story beyond a doubt, Queen Victoria made amends by giving him a gold snuff box. It didn't help him to clear his nostrils of the odium he had suffered, and he was more or less an Anglophobe till the day he died.

However, the reception of Mark Twain, in the wake of the departing Stanley, was a very different thing. For a century or so, the English had scorned American letters on the English model, and American scholarship on the German model. But —then as now—they never felt their dignity or status threatened by a comic character, especially if he excused himself from competitive gentility by coming out of the West. Mark Twain didn't know this. He came to England in 1872 with the intention of writing a satirical work about the English. He abandoned it in the downpour of adulation that rained on him. He was only thirty-seven. But he didn't have to call on anyone. The grandees came calling on him: the Lord Chancellor, Charles Reade, Canon Charles Kingsley. The Lord Mayor of London threw a banquet. Twain dutifully behaved like every gaping tourist he had satirized: off with his guidebook to the Abbey and St. Paul's, to Oxford and Stratford, only once breaking through this unusual reverential tone with the remark that the Albert Memorial was "the most genuinely humorous idea I have met with in this grave land."

He announced that "rural England is too absolutely beautiful to be left out of doors, it ought to be under a glass case." He took a daily walk along the King's Road finding "Shakespeare people all on hand as usual." England, he decided, had the prettiest, neatest, most competent maidservants in the world—a curious compliment from an egalitarian riverboat pilot and roving newspaperman.

He *was* taken aback by the poor districts of London, as Maxim Gorki was to be appalled by the poor of New York. But, then, travelers always notice the poor of other nations, because in their own country they have a regular daily itinerary, which doesn't take them for any sensible reason into the slums. In a foreign city, they tend to be footloose, and so are shocked by the waterfront of Marseilles, and the entrails of the Bowery, without ever having cause to investigate the lower depths of Glasgow or the interminable rotting wharves of the London river.

Mark Twain noticed also the general and, as he thought, nauseating deference towards royalty, and on a later visit he was to write blisteringly about it and blast away at the arrogance of empire. But on this first triumphal visit, the showers of flattery washed away his darker mood, and even when he meditated on the absurdity of noble titles, he did it jocosely: "All the dogs here," he wrote, "wear muzzles. Of course, they prefer it. Doubtless, some ducal dog wore one one day, because he had the toothache or for fun, and then the others adopted it."

The upshot of this visit was not a satire on England but a devastating denunciation of the United States. Surrounded in England by genial people of all classes, and a society disciplined, he fancied, by order and decorum, he thought back to the corruption of the South by the carpetbaggers, and the money-mania of the upstart buccaneers in tin, steel, copper, silver, the railroads. He thought of Boss Tweed and Jay Gould and what he called "an era of incredible rottenness"; and, in the glow of his Anglomania, he wrote *The Gilded Age.*

Well, you can't expect an Emerson or a Mark Twain every generation. And until the First World War, it is only fair to say that most Americans who committed themselves to print rehearsed themes so monotonous that the English, too, could recite them like nursery rhymes: the dankness of the climate, the greenness of the grass (a by-product of the climate), the rigid class distinctions, the tolerance of eccentrics from dotty parsons to village idiots; and the universal assumption of the English of all degrees that they were cock-of-the-walk, as, indeed—if you looked at a map and saw the quarter of the world colored in red—they were.

There are a couple of characteristics noted by all Americans of which, however, the English to this day appear to be unaware. One—first noticed in the Edwardian music halls and still remarkable in variety shows on television—is the curious English love of lavatory jokes. The other is the habit of paying agreeable Americans the insult—intended as a compliment—that they might well be mistaken for Englishmen.

What we don't find throughout the nineteenth century are the chronic American complaints about the discomforts of English life that provided all the main jokes of Americans in England between the First and Second World Wars. We don't find them because, it is now something of a shock to recall, the conditions of American life, for the traveler at any rate, were then more primitive still. At the beginning of the nineteenth century, Americans had learned to be on the defensive against just such a fussy visiting Englishman, and they were as haughty about him as the English came to be about the American tourist of the early twentieth century. Thus Washington Irving in 1820: "They miss some of the snug conveniences and petty comforts which belong to an old, highly-finished and over-populous state of society; where the ranks of useful labor are crowded, and many earn a painful and servile subsistence by studying the very caprices of appetite and self-indulgence. These minor comforts, however, are all-important in the estimation of narrow minds."

And through the middle of the century, English travelers in America—Mrs. Trollope, Thackeray, Dickens almost hysterically—went on about the brutal ordeal of travel by road or rail, about the heaviness of the fried food, its starchy monotony, the lack of vegetables, the frailty of the women, and the rheumy-eyed, long lean physique of the average American male. (Hence the cartoon symbol of Uncle Sam, who today would far better be represented by John Wayne or Jack Nicklaus.) So late as 1906, Baedeker's guide to the United States warned the visiting European that he must steel himself against hard beds, unvaried food, rutted roads, primitive inns, and cascades of public spitting. (The cuspidor, by the way, was—even forty years ago—a standard adjunct to every sofa and easy chair in an American hotel lounge.) But, Baedeker was quick to reassure you, it was worth all the hardship and the uncouthness in order to see the semi-tropical garden of the South, the brilliance of the New England fall, the wonders of Yosemite, the redwoods of California, etc., etc.

In the 1860s, it was Dickens in America who was put out to find that his shoes had not been polished overnight. In the

1940s, it was American infantrymen on duty in Alaska who complained about the lack of dry-cleaning facilities. I well remember being on a train—sometime in the early 1950s—that had gone through the Rockies and was entering the Utah Desert in the late afternoon. Suddenly, the train grew very stuffy, and a pretty sixteen-year-old girl, gold bracelets jangling on her wrist, began to clank up and down the corridors on her delicate high heels demanding to know why the air conditioning had given out. When I asked the conductor why he was in such a stew about this elegant brat, he said: "She'll raise hell in Salt Lake. Her grandfather started this railroad. The only difference between him and her is—he walked!"

It's only now clear that the 1930s, the forties, and the early fifties were the golden age of the American visitor's feeling of superiority to the Neanderthal life not of England alone but of all Europe. Europe had not then acquired, let alone improved on, the comforts of gadgetry—the refrigerators, cheap motorcars, cellophane wrappers, dial telephones, steam heat, room service, not to mention the later frozen foods, supermarkets, garbage dispose-alls—that abounded in America and made material life more comfortable for more people than ever before in human history. Middle-class Americans could come here and wallow in the complacency of bemoaning soggy vegetables, seedy hotels with fifteen-watt bulbs, warm cocktails, shivering houses, unworkable telephones, and Anglo-Saxon plumbing. In the late 1930s Margaret Halsey, in a funny book called *With Malice Toward Some,* was malicious toward everybody and everything in an English university town but generously conceded that when the rain cleared and the landscape turned its beautiful face toward you, like a naughty but enchanting woman, all was forgiven. For almost a decade after the Second War, this pleasurable feeling of superiority was compounded by the enforced shabbiness of economic austerity. It was a time when the American roving reporter A. J. Liebling could write: "An Englishman telling an

American about food is a case of the blind leading the one-eyed."

But in the thirty years since the Second War ended, this country has, I think, gone through a more marked social revolution than America. It is a shock to the new generation of traveling Americans, brought up on the advice of the old, to find that in some cities of the Midlands and the North, 50 and more percent of the schoolchildren were born in Asia or the West Indies; that the BBC's Sunday-morning news begins in Urdu; that, on the whole, public food is now at least as good in England as in America; that in pure scientific research England is comparatively superior, and in some branches of technology almost equally advanced; that all the gadgets of convenience, from freeways and supermarkets to cheap clothes off the peg and plastic wrapping, are now thoroughly domesticated; that America, the technological giant, settled too soon for a color television system that is glaringly inferior to either of the two European systems. All these things are unknown to most Americans of my generation who before, and just after, the Second War were able to come here and enjoy the pleasures of magnanimity in enduring mechanical inefficiency and clammy houses, and the snobbery and seediness of English life, while yet publicly declaring their affection for higher things—for the English landscape, royal and cathedral architecture, Savile Row tailoring, cucumber sandwiches, and English dogs. I know Americans of my age whose preconceptions about England are still firmly planted in the plays of Noel Coward, the life of country villages, the Foreign Office of Anthony Eden, the novels of Dorothy Sayers and P. G. Wodehouse, and the deep conviction that England may be high-toned but is touchingly amateur and invincibly undemocratic.

But, by a contradiction that afflicts every nation at some stage of its history, the more it develops a new character, the more it clings to the reputation of the old. There are Scotsmen who doggedly think of Edinburgh as a capital of world medicine. Vienna, that lugubrious city, gamely goes on marketing to intending tourists its legendary tradition of gaiety. There are Englishmen, and English newspapers, and even politicians, who still grow purple if anyone recalls the late Dean Acheson's twenty-year-old comment: "Britain has lost an empire and not yet found a role."

And, in the time we're talking about, when Americans were the world's most petted travelers, that was the last thing they wanted to be known as. They yearned to be thought of as simple, downright, no-nonsense democrats. And, as Franklin Roosevelt took the country out of its frontier innocence with swashbuckling irreverence, they found such a symbolic character, whose reputation as the All-American sage was undoubtedly inflated by the fact that he was a vanishing type.

He was part Cherokee Indian, born in Indian territory in what is now Oklahoma. He trailed herd. He bummed his way to New York and signed on as a night watchman for a shipload of sheep. He berthed briefly in London and sailed for Rio with a crew of cattle and on to India and South Africa. He broke in horses for the British army in the Boer War. Then on to Australia and New Zealand, and back to America. Footloose, and still only twenty-five, he showed off rope tricks at county fairs and then in Wild West shows, and wound up in, of all unlikely places, the Ziegfeld Follies. Within a few years, he was the favorite performer of presidents and kings: Will Rogers. He simply stood on a stage in his cowboy outfit and twirled a rope and said whatever was on his sassy mind.

To the delight of Americans, hugging their reputation as frontier wits in the moment of losing it, he was a sensation in England. For what Americans have rarely understood is that the best English instinct for what makes Americans admirable is a true one. The English might drop respectful nods in the direction of James Russell Lowell and Oliver Wendell Holmes, Edith

Wharton and Thornton Wilder, but before the American critics had made up their minds, it was the English critics who took the admiring measure of Bret Harte, and Walt Whitman, and Robert Frost. And at a time when New York and Boston looked on Mark Twain as a comic-strip buffoon, it was in England that he was first identified as the American Chaucer, and later—by Shaw—as the American Voltaire.

After Mark Twain, few Americans have been so welcomed as Will Rogers. The Prince of Wales took this wiry shambling cowboy, who had hair like a rope and a nose like a carrot, to Lord's to watch the cricket. They arrived at lunchtime, and Rogers had no sooner wakened from an afternoon nap than it was the tea interval. He said, "Your Royal Highness, if I ran this game, I'd line the players up at the start and say, Listen, fellas, no food till you're through." He twirled his rope at the command of George the Fifth and looked up at the royal box. "Your Majesty," he said, "you sure put on some great sights in London. But I wish you'd been with me on Saturday nights in Claremore, Oklahoma. Saturday night was the real thing . . . we used to go downtown to the barber shop and *watch haircuts!*"

This was all harmless, amiable stuff in a Mark Twain vein. But Rogers was no respecter of persons, or institutions, and like Twain he was a bitter skeptic about the honorable intentions of empires and top nations. He would, I suspect, have been murder on the adventure in Vietnam. Over forty years ago, he wrote: "This patriotic business is always the Big Brother helping the Weak Sister. . . . Sure, Japan and America and England can run countries perhaps better than China or Korea or India or the Philippines, but that don't mean they ought to. . . . I know men'd make my wife a better husband, but they ain't gonna get her." He looked at Abyssinia and her Italian conqueror: "As I see it, little nations has no business being little." These thoughts didn't issue from the Left or the Right. They came from the calm center of the hurricane, from a frontiersman who distrusted power and all hankerers after power. "One revolution," he wrote, "is just like one cocktail, it just gets you organized for the next." He looked at Russia: "Russia is a country that buries its troubles. Your criticism is your epitaph. You simply say your say, and then you're through." He looked at Wall Street and the City of London, when Samuel Insull was pyramiding holding companies for companies that were barely solvent. "A holding company," he said, "is the people you give your money to while you're being searched."

WE have not looked at one type of American who descends on this island from time to time not as a visitor but as a refugee: the conscious expatriate. They have come, in the past century, in three waves, and always on the pretext that America had become intolerably philistine. The generation of Henry James and Logan Pearsall Smith recoiled in horror from the vulgarity of the first industrial giants, from whom—in fact—most of the escapists derived their income and hence their freedom to shudder.

The second wave came, after the First World War, in ostensible protest against the crassness and frivolity of the American twenties. They too, however, returned mostly during the Depression, when their sudden loss of a remittance from home could be rationalized as a voluntary response to the courage and excitement of Roosevelt and the New Deal.

The third wave broke on this country in the last decade, when many high-minded Americans flocked to live in London on the claim that it was the last civilized city. On closer examination, these improbable *philosophes* turned out to be retired bankers, prosperous authors and screenwriters, and others, who had one pressing thing in common: the pressure of taxes at home and, if they came from New York City, a well-suppressed fear of street muggings and other random violence.

They stayed and reveled in London civilization until British inflation soared unreasonably, and the Labour Government began to hint at drastic changes in the tax laws. Since the maximum American federal tax on earned income remains at the beguiling limit of 50 percent, they have been beguiled into returning to the uncouth native shore. Thus began the second exodus of the disenchanted. Most of them are busy improvising plausible reasons for their return, for unlike the New Deal generation they cannot pretend that they are moved by the heroic arrival on the political scene of Gerald Ford.

Among this last wave is the fascinating case of S. J. Perelman, probably the most sophisticated American humorist of our time and, one might guess, a Platonic candidate for British citizenship, since more than any native Englishman he has mastered—as a weapon of parody—the exact vocabularies of practically every English writer from George Eliot to Conan Doyle, to Thomas Hardy and Evelyn Waugh. Money was never a consideration with Perelman, and his rapturous embrace of England and abrupt desertion of her were not allied to any melancholy induced by the inquisitiveness of the Inland Revenue. He left New York City, of which he is an archetypal native, with a withering blast at its dirt, garishness, advertising prose, con-man sycophancy, and nightly threats to life and limb. We were convinced he would never appear among us again.

He arrived in London describing himself—in a mockery of *Time* magazine prose—as "button-cute, wafer-thin, and pauper-poor." He was taken up by the wits and the intelligentsia of London as nobody since James Thurber. He wrote an hilarious account of his first hundred days, with a familiar but fresh emphasis on such mysteries as country weekends, judicial humor, and the bafflement of an electrician before an expired light bulb. He was very chic for a year or so, and then suddenly he was back in a small hotel room in downtown New York. He made a pass at such excuses as not being able—in England—to get dill pickles or rolls with sesame seeds in them. But he also confessed to the true reason. Unlike Henry James, he found England "too couth." More accurately, he said, "I can't explain to the English that we speak a different language. I miss the idiom." What he missed was his special native, New York, Jewish idiom of banter, irony, deadpan exaggeration; the wry, anarchic idiom of Groucho Marx, who was—by the way—as much a creation of Perelman's as of God's. For that invention alone, I think we may forgive him.

I have tried to sketch the private feelings of a few eminent Americans, and of many generations of anonymous Americans, to the experience of England as an alien country. There remains with us a conflict between the Englishman's private and public view of America which has been noticed from Emerson to our own time. Mark Twain put it bluntly: "All English individuals are kind and likeable—the newspapers are snobbish and pretentious, and they scoff at America. . . . English preachers and statesmen try to draw the two countries together in friendship and mutual respect—the newspapers, with what seems a steady and calculated purpose, discourage this. The newspapers are going to win this fight."

This conflict, between the Englishman's public and private view of Americans, is something, too, that Emerson, as usual, spotted with more subtlety and depth. "The English," he wrote in 1856, "like Americans but dislike the American structure of society, whilst yet [their] trade, mills, public education . . . are doing what they can to create in England the same social condition. America is the paradise of the [English] economists; is the favorite exception invariably quoted to the rules of ruin; but when he speaks directly of the Americans, the islander forgets his philosophy and remembers his disparaging anecdote."

In other words, ladies and gentlemen, except among the rare people whose preconceptions are whisked away by a free-wheeling intelligence, the original paranoia remains. After two hundred years of the father–prodigal son relationship, we all find it intolerable that we should not have firm, and usually uplifting, advice for each other. Whenever I hear or read a spontaneous anti-English remark, a brisk anti-American paragraph, I usually sense that a wild generalization is being made out of a single personal experience: the one-case induction method we all fall back on. The writer is exercising nothing more than the old stubborn refusal to be taken in.

We are all, I suspect, more often than we know, in the psychological situation of the old rabbi who was renowned among his congregation for his profound, though sometimes puzzling, maxims. On his deathbed, he said he wished to die in the temple. So he was taken there, and the congregation gathered in large numbers to catch from his dying lips the last pearl of his earthly wisdom. At last, he beckoned his assistant rabbi and panted out his final observation on the human condition. "Life," he said, "is like a barrel of water." And the phrase wafted like a zephyr through the long lines of the sorrowing flock: "Life is like a barrel of water, life is like a barrel of water." Till it came to the ears of the last little man in the line. Who said, "Life is like a barrel of water? But what does it mean?" And so the people muttered, and the phrase ran back again to the assistant rabbi, who leaned over the dying man and said, "Rabbi, the congregation is deeply moved by your remark, 'Life is like a barrel of water'—but they're asking, 'What does it mean?' " The old man lifted himself on one elbow. And he said, "So— it *isn't* like a barrel of water."

When all is said and done—when the politicians have mouthed their pious declarations of friendship and mutual dependence, when solemn educators have done trying to enlighten shrewd peasants, when the sociologists have staggered through the jungles of their polysyllables with the intention of discovering the roots of our life together, or apart; the fact is that much British writing about America, and American cogitations on the nature of England, spring still from the deep desire not to be unduly impressed by each other, and therefore to deliver a swift, bravura judgment, which is usually clever; but about which we might better say—as Alfred North Whitehead said to an admirer who found his theory of mathematics impressive—"Yes, I think it is. But the question is, is it also true?"

A NOTE ABOUT THE AUTHOR

Alistair Cooke was born in Manchester, England, and educated at Cambridge University, Yale, and Harvard. After serving for three years as the BBC's film critic, he settled in the United States in 1937, becoming an American citizen in 1941. For twenty-five years he was Chief American Correspondent of the *Manchester Guardian*.

Cooke's television history of America, a BBC production seen in thirty countries, was expanded into his greatly successful book *Alistair Cooke's America*. His commentaries on *Masterpiece Theatre* are seen by millions each week in the United States. But he is probably best known for his weekly BBC broadcast "Letter from America" which is heard in 52 countries and which, having marked its fortieth anniversary in March 1986, is far and away the longest-running radio series in broadcasting history. In 1973, for his "outstanding contribution over many years to Anglo-American mutual understanding," Queen Elizabeth made him an honorary Knight Commander of the British Empire.

Alistair Cooke lives in New York City and on Long Island, and is married to Jane White, the painter.

A NOTE ON THE TYPE

The text of this book was set in a digitized version of a type face known as Garamond. The design is based on letter forms originally created by Claude Garamond (c. 1480–1561). Garamond was a pupil of Geoffroy Tory and may have patterned his letter forms on Venetian models. To this day, the type face that bears his name is one of the most attractive used in book composition, and the intervening years have caused it to lose little of its freshness or beauty.

Composed by David E. Seham Associates, Inc., Metuchen, New Jersey.
Printed and bound by R. R. Donnelley & Sons, Harrisonburg, Virginia.
Typography and binding design by Iris Weinstein